Releasing Alexandra

The Memoir of a Woman Who Set Herself Free

Sandra & Lee J. Everitt

ACKNOWLEDGMENTS

I want to thank God for the blessings I've known in this life. The biggest blessings of all are the people I've known and loved. They've included friends, loved ones, and all the members in the mob of characters that today make up our family. However, I want to especially acknowledge my father, Dale Bramlett. What an encourager he was for his overly anxious, shy third daughter. Being with him, when I was growing up, let me find a haven from the anxiety I dealt with so often. Only his uplifting words seemed to calm my mind when I was a child. Later, as an adult I mimicked his salesmanship techniques and became quite a successful salesperson in my own right.

I also want to recognize my mother, Evelyn Bramlett. She was selfless to a fault when it came to her family. She worked tirelessly for me and my three sisters. I've tried to model myself after her in the way I've raised our three daughters. Mother expected each of us to do the best we were capable of. She believed that expectations from a parent was a necessary part of being a successful parent. She was a successful parent for all her daughters.

Lastly, I want to recognize the wonderful man I've made my life's journey with. Together we've co-authored this book. He's had a big part in helping me discover things about myself I never knew even existed. He was the one who gave that hidden part of me a name when she began to emerge after we were married. His suggestion was that we name her Alexandra. The name stuck and is now a part of the title to this treatise. Thanks for the memories, honey!

CONTENTS

PROLOGUE

As I watched the kids "help" Lee J. load the car with our supplies for a picnic day at the beach, I had no clue that this day, on a secluded beach in Florida, I would remember for a lifetime. In less than an hour, I would find myself—a shy, overly anxious twenty-four-year-old wife and mother from a small town in Texas—walking down a beach in broad daylight with my boobs totally uncovered, **and I would feel wonderful about it!** A previously unknown persona inside me would have the opportunity to really emerge in "public" for the first time. Of course, in this case, "public" refers to just my husband and our two young daughters.

Shortly, we added the lunch I'd prepared to the beach stuff the kids and their dad had already put in the car and drove the short distance to the beach parking area. We parked where we always did when we were going to the dunes area, where I liked to sunbathe. But today, we walked on past that area and just kept going. The only sign of people having been there were a few dune buggy tracks. We were taking it pretty slow so the kids could keep up. Lee J. had mentioned earlier that the beach had no public ground access to it since it was owned by the Air Force. One could only walk to it as we were doing.

Upon reaching, it appeared we were the only people there. It really did seem to be secluded, so finally, I could hold it no longer. I blurted out and asked Lee J., "What would you think if I told you I wanted to go topless for the day?"

I suppose it was the newly found confidence and decrease in my anxiety and shyness that were showing through because the idea of going topless was strictly something I'd conjured up on my own. At the time, my motivation was simple. I wanted to erase some tan lines I considered "unattractive."

My question caught Lee J. by surprise and initially, he thought I was kidding, but then he soon realized I was not. He quickly said, "If that's what you want to do, I will certainly enjoy the scenery."

I smiled inwardly but didn't say anything else for a minute or two. My heart was pounding as once more I looked around and convinced myself we really were on a very secluded beach. This was a huge step for me. I took a deep breath, slipped my shoulder straps off, and pushed my top down to my waist. For the first time ever, I was naked from the waist up on a public beach. As I said to start this narration, **it felt wonderful.** Lee J. was pretty much speechless. We walked just a few steps further when I thought, *What the heck!* I unhooked my top from around my waist, pitched it to him, and said, "Just put it in the beach bag; I don't think I'll wear it today."

He grinned and complied as we continued our walk. I had just embraced a new sensual feeling I'd never known before. A kind of inner euphoria started to envelop me. Later, Lee J. would tell me how he was totally fascinated by my behavior which was both crazy and unusual for me.

How had I gotten to this place where I could push aside my lifelong affliction of high-functioning anxiety and almost debilitating shyness and do something that was totally outrageous for me? For the last three months, we had been living in Mexico Beach, Florida, where we had rented a small beach house. We were 1,100 miles from home. Lee J. was going through a four-month course of F-106 training just down the road at Tyndall AFB. The kids and I were truly "living the dream." Early on in his training, he was gone Monday through Friday during the day while the girls and I spent most of the day on the beach. What a time we all had been having! At the time, Julie was five and Angie was three. We had taken to the beach life in a big way.

The mores of our small hometown in Texas, where I had grown up, didn't seem applicable to the beach life I was experiencing in Florida. The biggest difference was my attire. Though I was innately shy, I did love to wear some things that were a little daring. I had bought a couple of skimpy bikinis and made several halter and short sets for myself and the kids. Things of that nature had become my principle attire for the summer. Skimpy swimwear was not common for someone my age back in my hometown of Idalou, Texas. Nevertheless, I loved the feel of the sun and fresh air on my mostly uncovered body, but my actions that day would push the envelope even more.

I thought I was wearing only my bikini bottoms, but as Lee J. would later tell me, I also was wearing the most mischievous, smirky grin on my face that he had ever seen. As we continued to walk, I saw that he couldn't keep his eyes off me. I could feel the jiggle of my breasts as we walked, and more than once, I teasingly turned toward him and accentuated the jiggles even more. I could see I was driving him crazy. Such fun!

We soon found a suitable spot to have our picnic, so we stopped and spread out our beach paraphernalia. It was late morning by now, and the girls and I were just wading and playing in the shallow surf. Lee J. had made himself comfortable on the beach and was just watching us. I felt his gaze upon me and smiled inwardly. I was feeling like a bird that had been let out of its cage. I became more and more exhilarated.

I would spend the whole afternoon without the top of my bikini. I'd never felt a freedom quite like this. Though I was not a drinker, it was like I was intoxicated because I definitely didn't care how close to being naked I was there on that beach with just Lee J. and our girls. The kids never seemed to notice that their mother didn't have her top on. I think the fact that there was a lot of casual nudity in our normal household probably had something to do with it.

After eating our lunch, we all went out in the shallow surf once more. There, we both played with the kids for a while, but I was well aware that my husband's eyes were constantly upon me. More than once, out of sheer mischievousness, I gave him a provocative look and a jiggle with a little smirk to go with it. Again, the kids never noticed anything, of course, they were only five and three years old. His only reaction was an approving grin. I was really enjoying the effect I was having on him.

I wanted to sunbathe, so Lee J. stayed and played with the kids for a while longer as I went back to where our towels were laid out. Later, he walked back to where I was sunbathing and sat down by me. He immediately asked, "What's going on inside your head?"

My responses seemed to leave him even more perplexed. The first thing I told him was that lately, I had been having some of the strangest feelings inside me, just below the surface. I was feeling like I both wanted and **needed** to do something for myself that was spontaneous and outrageous. The idea of going topless on the beach seemed to meet that criteria. Initially, my motivation was simply to ditch my bikini top so I could get rid of some unwanted tan lines, but as I related earlier, I soon found that a kind of euphoria had enveloped me. I added that shortly after I removed my top, the thought of spending the rest of the day semi-naked with him and the kids on a beach over 1,100 miles from home became irresistible. **Not since our honeymoon had I felt this kind of freedom.** It seemed to release some emotional issues I'd had for as long as I could remember. I went on to tell him I thought that this mental weight I'd been carrying was left over from my years growing up under my mother's tight rein. My actions that day would have never been met with her approval, yet he had embraced them. His approval in itself was liberating.

I continued, and as I told him on a much lighter note, I was finding I really liked the sensation of my breasts being exposed to the fresh air and sunlight. It was both refreshing and invigorating. Then, I somewhat sarcastically mentioned that it appeared that he was enjoying (as he called it) the scenery I was providing. Though I didn't tell him verbally, I had to admit that I, too, was enjoying my effect on him. For me, teasing him like that felt empowering, but I could tell my responses to his earlier question had left him still somewhat baffled. It would take a while for both of us to fully comprehend what was going on inside me.

A while later, we continued our conversation and reminisced a bit about how our seventh anniversary was coming up the following month. We talked about the two beautiful little girls we had made as we watched them play there on the beach in the sand. Lee J. opened up even more when he told me what a wonderful mom he thought I was for our girls and, in the same breath, how he was so proud to have me for such a wonderful wife and incredible lover. **It was very humbling to hear those words.** He leaned over, kissed me quite tenderly, and then walked back down to where the kids were playing.

As I lay there sunbathing, I thought about the past three months and how it had been such an incredible time for both of us. His training had taken him to a place he couldn't have imagined two years earlier when **we'd** joined the Air Force. I'd spent the last three months on a perpetual beach vacation that had absolutely awakened something inside me. I had always loved being outdoors and had grown up lying out in our backyard sunbathing with my sisters. During our early weeks in Florida, I had worked to become very fit and toned, and I now had a very deep tan. Lee J. told me quite often how beautiful he thought I was, and in turn, I tried to look my best for him. I have to admit, by now, I was really proud of the way I looked. To be quite honest, I had become somewhat vain. That was something I was taught by my mother to avoid.

Early on in our stay there, I realized that I did garner attention on the beach and elsewhere. One day, I said something about it to Lee J. He told me it was really quite simple. On the beach and elsewhere, I was seen as a sexy, beautiful young woman. It was obvious I was married and had two kids since they were always with me. I suppose his explanation enlightened me somewhat. I continued to be keenly aware of the attention the kids and I were receiving, and I really loved it. What woman wouldn't!

During these past weeks, I felt I had done nothing that could be considered outrageous or flaunting. In fact, most of the other young women on the beach wore pretty much the same kinds of attire I did. Yet, one of the mantras that had been drilled into me and my sisters by our mother had become a burden lurking in the background of my psyche. Growing up, Mother told us, "Never toot your own horn, and never do anything that might cause the neighbors to talk."

She was appalled at anyone who ever bragged about themselves whether it be verbally or visually. Something inside me from those years under her tutelage subconsciously made me think that looking the way I did and wearing minimal swimwear in such a public place as the beach was a way of bragging about myself. It left me conflicted!

I was starting to realize I was enduring some psychological tension stemming all the way back to my childhood. The more I thought about it as I lay there sunbathing, the more I realized I had a lot going on just beneath the surface, and until that day, I'd kept it pretty well hidden from everybody, even Lee J. My behavior earlier that day seemed to have changed everything or at the very least, had started to change everything!

I had been born with a nature that made me exceedingly shy, and I was prone to be overly anxious about anything and everything. I later learned it was called "high functioning anxiety." Add to that, even though I had gotten married and left home seven years earlier, subconsciously, I was still adhering to my mother's two mantras. I continued to carry a lot of emotional baggage I had accumulated while growing up. Yet here I was, sunbathing almost naked on a "public" beach with my kids and my husband, and I felt nothing but euphoria and freedom like I'd never before experienced. I had pushed aside my natural shyness and anxiety and had possibly broken both of my mother's rules that day, and **I felt wonderful about it all.**

I think that day was the day I started to get past needing anyone's approval for my actions (other than my husband's) ever again. I also think as I lay there sunbathing topless, I figuratively thumbed my nose at the innate shyness and overanxiousness I had dealt with my entire life. I was neither anxious nor shy about my actions that day. I'm sure there may have been even more to what I was feeling, but for the time being, I was satisfied with my realization of what was going on inside me. I learned my psychological issues were far greater than I had ever realized. It was the start of a process that would take quite some time to sort it all out.

It was nearing midafternoon when Lee J. came back and sat down beside me again. He said it appeared to him that I had an unbridled happiness that seemed to flow from me. He described my demeanor as nothing less than giddy, and he had never witnessed that in me in such a manner before. He told me that I appeared deliriously happy! I was. He then grinned and asked me what had happened to that bashful, shy young girl he had started dating ten years earlier.

He had seen glimpses of this new behavior from me from time to time, such as on our honeymoon, but this was the first time I'd shown a totally new persona that was such a radical departure from what was my norm. He then added that though I had surprised him and left him somewhat confused earlier, he really liked this new side of me. He then commented that I was doing nothing wrong; it was just our little family there on that beach, and he was loving every minute of it. Then he added something that most assuredly tugged at my heartstrings. He said he thought maybe he had fallen a little deeper in love with me that day. Those words made me wonder if he even knew what he was feeling. *Was it love or lust?* After all, I had been almost naked with him for most of the day. Either way, I thought his words were very sweet. His acceptance of my explanations about what I was dealing with left me with the confidence to continue exploring these new underlying emotional demands.

We spent the rest of that afternoon playing with the kids and continuing our conversation. He didn't seem to be able to take his eyes off me. **What a feeling!** That day would become a most memorable time for both of us; it was a time we both continue to remember vividly, even today. During the previous weeks, I had learned to love the feel of the sun and wind on my mostly bare body, but that day had been an entirely new experience. Even more of me had been fully exposed, and I mean that in both a physical and psychological way. As I said earlier, "I felt like the bird that had been let out of its cage."

As we started our walk back to the car, I was still feeling the new freedom I'd experienced that day, but I wondered to what degree I would continue to feel this way the next day and days beyond. It was an unknown for me as we walked. Then, Lee J. reminded me that he still had three more weeks of training left and asked if I wanted to have additional opportunities similar to what I had experienced that day. Of course, I said, "Yes!"

As we neared the dunes area, I knew I had to get my top from the beach bag and put it on again. When I could wait no longer, I reluctantly did so. It was then I noticed my breasts were not as completely tanned as the rest of my body, but they were certainly not lily white anymore, either. They would become completely tanned before we left Florida three weeks later.

Somewhere during our return to the parking lot, Lee J. jokingly told me my new persona needed a name. I had given something like that absolutely no previous thought, but he obviously had. As we continued our walk back to the car, he said, "Let's call her Alexandra."

I thought, *Why not!* It was similar to my given name, Sandra, but little did I know it would stick, and even today, it is used by our family to describe the more free-spirited side of my personality. I would continue to feel this newly expanded "Alexandra" personality emerge more and more, but it would actually take quite some time to complete. That Saturday in June of 1971 turned out to just be the beginning of "releasing Alexandra."

Who Am I and Where Did I Come From

I know the title above may seem a little strange, but I liked it because it allowed me to use a phrase with a double meaning. The first meaning is simple and very straightforward. It deals with the historical facts of my childhood, however, the second meaning deals with the psychological side of some internal issues I faced. That became a very real problem for me as I will relate later. For now, I'll just lay out the historical facts of my early childhood.

I was born on November 11, 1946, in Dublin, Texas, to Dale and Evelyn Bramlett. I was the third of their four daughters. My two older siblings were Barbara Ann (Barb) and Brenda Joy. My younger sister was Kathy Evelyn. My early childhood was spent in Dublin in a neighborhood full of other kids. The environment for us was quite normal for the times. Our births were spread over a ten-year period, with three or four years between each of us. The fact we were a family of all girls meant there could always be a certain amount of drama about almost anything in our household. (It must be a girl thing.)

Of course, I don't have any early memories of myself, only stories about me from my oldest sister Barb who was seven years my senior. She describes me as someone who couldn't keep her pants pulled up. They just seemed to always be hanging on just below my chubby belly. She says she was constantly pulling them up but to little avail. She describes me as a normal, happy preschooler.

From the pictures available, I was a chubby little ragamuffin. Both of my older sisters were dark-headed, but I was as towheaded as they come. This was to become a factor for some mental issues on my part later in my childhood. It seemed to me that people didn't seem to know that I was a part of the Bramlett household.

During this time, my dad was employed by the veteran's school in Erath County, Texas, but in the spring of 1952, that job was over. Coincidentally, an opportunity to move to the plains of West Texas presented itself. My dad's brother helped him secure a job with the John Deere equipment dealership in Lubbock, Texas, starting in June of 1952. My folks found a house in Lubbock that they rented for the summer after the move from Dublin.

During that first summer in Lubbock, Daddy applied to several local schools for a teaching position and soon had offers from both Idalou and Roosevelt. Mother wanted him to have a job in a school system that was part of a town. Since Roosevelt was a country school, Idalou was a no-brainer in that regard; Idalou became our home. We left Lubbock and moved to Idalou at the start of that school year.

The move to West Texas was not without some drama, though. Barb would enter the 7th grade in the fall of 1952 and leaving Dublin was traumatic for her. She was leaving the only home she had ever known and the friends she was sure she could not live without. However, being Barb, she soon found new friends in Idalou, and all became well in her world. After just two weeks, she said she loved being in Idalou.

I stayed at home with Mother and my baby sister, Kathy, during our first year in Idalou since there was no public kindergarten back then. My sisters and I would play school, and for whatever reason, they treated me like the village idiot. I can remember getting mostly D's and F's on my papers they graded. However, I was very prepared to start school, probably far better prepared than most of my peers. Barb tells the story of Mother quizzing me after my first day of school. She asked me what I had learned at school that day, and, the story is, I said, "Well, nothing! Those idiots (presumably my classmates) don't even know how to read!" I guess even though I got bad grades from my sisters in their play school, I was able to learn enough to read pretty well before I started real school.

And so began my school years. But first, I must say that I never enjoyed school, **ever**. Even though I had no trouble being an excellent student, my constant anxiety from not knowing what the teacher would do next, afraid of being called on in front of the class, and shyness that was almost painful made school, at the very least, quite unpleasant for me.

It was when I started school that my anxiety issues came to the forefront. Even though I experienced anxiety at home, it ramped up considerably when I started school. In later years, I would learn that I had what psychologists call "high functioning anxiety." It is not a mental illness as such, but through some research on the internet, I've learned it can definitely take a toll on a person's mental health. It unquestionably took a toll on mine. I also learned it can have a genetic component. In my case, I'm sure I inherited it from my daddy. He dealt with high anxiety his entire life, especially when the issue causing his anxiety dealt with his family.

I've previously stated I was exceedingly shy, which my research has told me, too, can have a genetic component. In the case of my shyness, I inherited that from my mother. When my shyness was coupled with my anxiety, it was a recipe for me to never enjoy my school days, even though I was always an excellent student.

From reading some material on how high-functioning anxiety manifests itself in different people, I've learned that I was affected by at least four different psychological issues.

1) **I had persistent feelings of worry, fear, and uneasiness.** I constantly worried about everything.

2) **I had a desire for perfection.** Good grades were expected from all of us in our family, but I honestly never remember being told explicitly by either Mother or Daddy what was expected as far as my grades were concerned. I knew I was smart, and I knew I should make A's. I suppose I put pressure on myself to excel, but I can't say what level my mother truly expected. Whatever the expectations were, I mostly made A+'s and A's.

3) **I could never relax completely.** My mind was constantly worrying about whatever the next thing

involving schoolwork was going to entail.

4) **I overthought everything.** I would constantly go over assignments again and again. I tended to just pick them to death.

I remember an example of what I was dealing with came from my mother. One of the most unpleasant experiences during my time in elementary school happened in the third grade. My third-grade teacher's daughter was also in her mother's classroom that year. For some reason, my teacher seemed to intensely dislike me. Looking back on it now, the only rational reason for her disliking me was that I was a threat to her daughter. I was no threat physically. (I was afraid of my own shadow.) Moreover, I hardly even talked to her daughter. Her dislike for me had to have been a jealousy thing; I got better grades than her daughter did, and truthfully, I was prettier.

One day, I had a note from the teacher to take home to Mother. It accused me of saying something bad about a little girl in the class who had a speech impediment. **Her daughter had totally made it up.** I knew that I had never said anything remotely bad about the other little girl. In fact, I was one of the few friends she had. I promised Mother that I had never said anything about the other little girl, much less something bad. (That was not my nature then, nor is it my nature now.) Yet Mother got really mad at me and said she didn't believe I hadn't done anything. She then admonished me not to do it again. I didn't argue; in fact, I can't remember arguing with Mother about anything, **ever**. It just was not my nature.

Though my feelings had been hurt and my anxiety was soaring, I did what Mother always told me to do when something was troubling me, "Get over it." So I did. Her words certainly didn't make my life easier, but they did make me tougher. Mother just did not know what to do with me because I was so different from my older sisters. I kept my emotions to myself, which was quite unlike both my older sisters. Barb would argue, Brenda showed her anger, and I showed nothing. I just went to my room.

There was no doubt about Mother's love for all of us. Her whole life revolved around her family. She was selfless to a fault. She literally worked seven days a week during the years when we were all at home. Just keeping us fed was a full-time job. In the summertime, we helped her can enormous amounts of food for our use during the winter. In addition to all of that, she made all our clothes. My memory of her was that she worked pretty much all the time.

Everything she did was a labor of love for us, but she had four very different daughters. I was the one she understood the least. But you don't have to understand someone to love them, and I knew that Mother loved me even when I didn't understand her reaction to the incident described above. I think, however, I became both a tough and sweet little kid. (If you don't make waves, you're generally considered sweet.) I know suppressing my emotions as a child was a definite fact in my life. It would be years before those pent-up emotions would find a release, but find a release they eventually did.

There was another incident that occurred when I was in the third or fourth grade of elementary school. It happened at a high school football game and has stuck in my memory all these years. To preface the description of the incident, I should mention that I was kind of invisible to a lot of people. I was bashful and wanted no attention; several times, I heard someone say, "Whose little girl is this?" It made me wonder why I didn't seem to belong to my own family. It irritated Mother to no end when she heard it, and it undoubtedly increased my anxiety to the point of wondering if I really belonged there. (*Was I adopted or something?*) Barb and Brenda even joked a little about me being "adopted." I know they were just teasing me, but I truly did wonder why no one could see I was a part of the Bramlett family. Again these emotions just got suppressed like so many others.

I think you can see why I used the "Where did I come from?" phrase in the title of this chapter. The culmination of all this happened at a football game when an errant football from the field came sailing into the stands. It hit me right in the face. I wasn't hurt badly, but it scared me to death, and of course, I started crying. I was sitting a row or two in front of Mother, and once again, someone said, "Whose little girl is this?"

Mother very indignantly replied, "Why, she's ours!"

I think it really had started to bother her a lot and again, it really **bothered** me. It ramped up my already high anxiety even more. I think as I look back, the fact that my two older sisters were dark-headed and I was a blondie made it hard for people to make the connection that we were sisters. Add to that, Kathy was redheaded, and I can understand the confusion. It certainly was upsetting to me at the time.

I suppose as I moved on up in elementary school, I gradually realized I really was part of my family. However, early on, that absolutely had not been the case. It was just one more piece of accumulated psychological baggage I would bear into my adulthood. Though carrying quite a burden inside myself, I was learning to get through it solely on my own. I learned to hide and suppress my emotions quite well. It would be after meeting Lee J. that I would find a way to start releasing a lot of the emotional baggage I had accumulated during my childhood years. It would be after I got married and left home. Only then would I begin to realize just how heavy the subconscious mental burden was that I was carrying!

At home, I supposedly was a model child. In fact, Barb says that as a child, "I was perfect!" She goes on to tell the tales of the sibling conflict in our house. Her quote goes something like this. "I fought with Brenda, Brenda fought with me, Brenda fought with Kathy, Brenda fought with Mother, and Sandy fought with no one! If some conflict started, Sandy just ran down the hall and disappeared into her room. I don't remember her ever getting a spanking."

Wow! When I look back at the words in that quote and think a bit, I realize that that's my recollection, too. I hated conflict and avoided it whenever possible. My main coping mechanism was to suppress whatever emotion I was feeling and then **withdraw** from the situation. I was probably too young to even know how to verbalize what I was dealing with. I do remember as I got older, though, I might say something to Barb or Daddy about it, but mainly I coped by withdrawing into myself. I could lose myself in a book, and that would get me through whatever was going on. In fact, I read *Gone With the Wind* for the first time when I was about 8. I think I finally read through it completely at least three times, maybe more.

As I alluded to previously, my mother was a hard worker and Daddy was so proud of her ability to manage their household. But he was a hard worker, too. It seemed like he was always working. Invariably, he would find some kind of extra job to make more money. He sold encyclopedias, vacuum cleaners, and such. He was a consummate salesman. He was truly interested in getting to know his customers. Most people looked forward to seeing him come by from time to time. He had a great memory, and he would ask questions about the customers' families and other details that he remembered from the last time he had talked to them. He sold a lot of "stuff" because of his personality, and he had great fun doing it. He truly was a people person and enjoyed his side sales jobs immensely. He used to let me go with him, and I subconsciously learned some of his sales techniques that would serve me well in years to come.

When I was six or seven years old, Daddy started letting me walk with him to get the mail. He loved to walk, and getting the mail was a good excuse to get some exercise since there was no home delivery of our mail back during those days. I remember how he would walk slowly so I could keep up. We would just walk and talk. He loved to joke with me, and he could always make me laugh. I think maybe some of my answers made him laugh, too. It was always such a happy time for me. I now know that getting to go with him to get the mail was a form of withdrawal from my normal world of shyness and high anxiety. In fact, when I was very young, if he got off without me, I would be crushed and would cry. Being with Daddy was my safe place. I have such fond memories of being with him during this time of my life.

As I have said before, Daddy was always looking for ways to provide more income for his family. He drove a school bus for extra money every school day. Rather than going home after school, some days, I would go with him and ride his bus. I would ride up front close to him. Looking back, I see these times as a way for me to leave my world of excessive shyness and overanxiety behind once again, if only temporarily. I think it could have been some sort of babysitting he did to help Mother out. Either way, I loved being with him by myself.

In the summertime, I would tag along as he worked on his summer job measuring crops for the USDA. By the time I was eleven or twelve, he would take me with him because I really could help him speed up his job. Without going into great detail, instead of walking off all his measurements with the measuring wheel, he would have me drive the car while he rolled the measuring wheel by riding on the fender. I actually learned to drive at an early age because of this. But most of all, I loved it because of the time we got to spend together when he would talk and maybe tease me a little; my anxiety level would become basically nonexistent. Daddy would even break one of Mother's mantras and brag on all of his girls; he was such an encourager. I always thought I might be his "favorite" because he really liked that I loved to tag along with him so much. Being with him always let me push my anxiety aside for a time, and everyone in the family said I was a younger "girl version" of my daddy. For whatever reason, I really was a lot like him. And again, how I always loved being with him. I still miss him even today.

As a side note on the subject of the time I got to spend with Daddy, Lee J. once told me he'd read about a study that looked at marriages where the wife came from a family with a nurturing father figure as opposed to the wife coming from a family where the opposite was true. The conclusions from the study found that husbands whose wives came from a home with a nurturing father figure were more than twice as likely to view their wives as a great mother for their kids and a great friend and a lover. Lee J. has kidded me through the years that he has my daddy to thank for the fact we've had such a great sex life. He's told me many times throughout our lives together how he has always considered me a great mother for our kids and a great lover for him. I always smile when he says that because even though it sounds kind of funny, it's also very sweet.

Tagging along with Daddy gave me a lot of one-on-one time with him that I never got with my mother. I remember the only time I considered personal time with her was when she took a bath. It wasn't just me and her; it was all of us girls. We would gather around the tub and have a wonderful conversation with her. (This was a custom I took with me when I had my own family of girls years later.) There's just something about having a captive audience with the naked lady in the tub. Everybody got their chance to talk. Granted, it was not a solitary one-on-one time, but it was "quality time." It really was true family time for us girls, though it happened in an environment some people might consider to be somewhat unusual.

We did have most of our meals together, so our family time with Daddy present was around the dinner table. An anecdote from our meal times that illustrates the type of person Mother was, was concerned about her "love" for fried chicken necks. Before the days of "chicken strips," she would cut up a whole chicken. We girls could be quite ravenous, each reaching for our favorite part of the chicken. She always chose the neck. It doesn't take a rocket scientist to figure out that she chose the neck because none of us wanted it. She wanted us to get what we wanted. When it came to us, she was selfless!

Like most mothers, the baby of the family sometimes gets treated a bit differently than the kids that came before them. Mother was no different. Of course, my younger sister Kathy was the baby of our family, and **Kathy had red hair and**

freckles. Mother hated those freckles, but we all thought she had the most beautiful dark red auburn hair you could imagine. But between the freckles and being the baby of the family, Mother cut Kathy some slack, and we all thought she babied her some.

Meanwhile, I tended to gravitate towards hanging out with my older sisters because, to me, Kathy was the "baby." I think the fact Barb and Brenda treated me as an equal, and I was never as close to Kathy as I was to my two older sisters. Being with them was where I wanted to be, and it kind of pushed my maturity along ahead of my years.

I do recognize, however, that being the baby of the family does generally cut that child some slack from their parents. I know when our last child, Marnie, was born, **I just felt tired.** It was easier to let some things slide rather than be as rigid with her as I was with our first two children, Julie and Angie. I realize now that Mother babying Kathy was something quite normal in a lot of families. At the time, though, it was just another one of those things I pushed down and filed away with all the other stuff I had previously buried deep inside my psyche.

Mother also had some very different rules for us kids to abide by. It was much later in my life when I thought about how weird some of her rules might seem to other kids. When we were very young, we could have all the neighborhood kids over to our yard to play, but we were not allowed to go over and play in their yards. Daddy was very protective of his gaggle of girls, but it fell on Mother to be the enforcer. I think she thought if everyone was at our house, she would remain in control. I guess the neighborhood kids just accepted that stipulation. I remember a lot of playtime with the other kids, and it was always in our yard. It was the same in both Dublin and Idalou. It definitely was a happy time for me, but upon reflection, it did seem a little weird.

Early on, I learned about my mother's two mantras, as we called them. As I alluded to in the prologue, they were:

1) Never "toot your own horn!"

2) Never do anything that would make the neighbors talk! (Although, as weird as most of our neighbors were, I wondered why she even cared.)

I think because of my shy nature, I self-inflicted a lot of pressure on myself to never say or do anything that would violate either of those rules. Regardless of where the pressure I felt came from, living by those rules kept my anxiety and shyness issues quite high a lot of the time. I learned to just stay under the radar by being quiet and minding my own business.

Mother was aware that I dealt with a lot of anxiety and had an innate shy nature, but she cut me no slack. I never talked to her about it, and if she sensed I was dealing with some issue, her words were simply, "Get over it!" It wasn't that she didn't love me. I don't think she ever truly understood my anxiety issues because she wasn't a particularly anxious person. Though she was "reserved" and had been shy as a kid herself, I was different. I did not want attention drawn to myself, so **I just got tougher.** It would serve me well in later life with my own kids.

Mother was my role model when I became a mother, but I vowed to try to give my kids more personal time than I got from her, and I do think I was successful in that area with my three kids, but there were differences. Mother had four of us to deal with, and I only had three. Additionally, life was harder as a mother when I was growing up. My life certainly wasn't as hard as hers, so I was able to give more one-on-one time to my kids.

I always had a bond with Barb and Brenda. Though I shared a room with Kathy, she was always a baby to me, and as I've said earlier, Mother seemed to treat her as such. So, it was Barb, Brenda, and me, and then there was Kathy. Through all the years our "sisterhood" never included her. I loved the fact that the three of us could talk. Even though I was seven years younger than Barb and four years younger than Brenda, they always treated me as an equal as I got older. Barb would tell anyone that I always seemed older than my years. She and Brenda started letting me go with them when they went "riding around the drag." I gave them no trouble, and I loved being with their older friends. This, being older than my years, accelerated when I entered junior high.

So, how do I sum up who I was by the time I was about to enter junior high school? I suppose I do have Mother to thank for me learning to live with my anxiety and shyness, but I also have her to thank for those feelings being as intense as they were. Mother treated us all the same, but I internalized them more than my sisters. As I got older during my time in elementary school, I gradually got tougher. I had no one to guide me; I simply did it by myself. I did learn much later that I had an enormous amount of things pent-up inside me that would begin to emerge after I left home when Lee J. and I got married. In fact, that emergence is what this book is about. It was quite a ride. Hang on!

MINDING MY OWN BUSINESS

It was a sunny Sunday afternoon in the summer of 1985 or 1986 when Daddy made a statement to Lee J. that thrilled me then and still thrills me today. Barb's husband, Dan, and Lee J. both moved out to the front porch of my folk's house after finishing a family lunch that Sunday. Daddy soon joined them. It was a habit for them to go out on the front porch to have one of their wide-ranging discussions of almost anything from politics to the weather. My daddy loved talking to his sons-in-law, and Lee J. especially loved those times with him.

Out of nowhere, Daddy suddenly made a statement about me. He said, **"That Sandy is something, isn't she?"** I know that these words would be quite an unremarkable statement if you didn't know the background from which they came. I'm also aware that the time period for this chapter is a long way away from where I left off in the last chapter. It's actually a jump of over twenty-five years, so follow along as I fill in the gaps of why this was such a special statement from my daddy about me.

Daddy came from a very poor, rural background in Erath County, Texas. His parents couldn't give him much in the way of worldly things, but they did give him an intense desire for learning. It took him quite some time, with several stops and starts, to get his college degree, but he did eventually attain it. He desperately wanted to make sure all of his girls had the opportunity to attend college. Both Barb and Brenda started college right out of high school, just like he'd hoped. But when I came along, my wishes and his wants collided.

You see, Daddy's quiet, overanxious, bashful third daughter had gone off the rails and fallen in love with a farm boy, Lee J. Everitt, who was three years older than me. We'd started dating when I was just fourteen years old. He was entering his senior year in high school as I was beginning my freshman year. Three years is not much of a difference when you're in your twenties or older, but it's quite a difference for two teenagers. We were the classic example of a teenage romance back in the early sixties.

I'll tell more about our dating years later, but for now, I'll skip ahead to the time just prior to my graduation from high school.

It was during my sophomore year that I had to have the "talk" with Mother and Daddy about me getting out of high school in three years. Mother was okay with it, but Daddy...not so much. I wanted to get married. My plan was simple: to graduate from high school in three years to get married and start my life with Lee J. To be perfectly honest, our passion for each other was off the charts. Three years of dating was a long time, and the desire I felt had nothing to do with getting a college degree. I only wanted to be with him, and I told Daddy that, unlike both of my older sisters, I had no desire to pursue a college degree of any kind. **I also didn't** want to become a teacher like my elder siblings. I clarified to him I wanted to be like Mother, to be a housewife and raise a family. He argued that I was so smart that not getting a college degree was a waste of my talent. His desires didn't change my mind, though.

As I was graduating high school in three years, I was technically not a member of the class I started high school with or a member of the class I was graduating with. However, my grades were such that I would have been the valedictorian of either class had I taken a more traditional route to graduation. I had to tell Daddy that I didn't want to put my life on hold to get a degree that I neither wanted nor planned to use. **That was the day I sorely disappointed him.** I was deeply saddened for "letting him down," but I was sure that Lee J. and I were destined to have a happy life together. We had our difficulties through the years, but overall, our marriage has been happy and quite satisfying.

For the next twenty years or so, I happily lived in the shadow of my husband. He became an Air Force fighter pilot, and that made me an officer's wife for five years. During his assignment in Montana, our third daughter, Marnie Jae, was born. Our family was now complete. What adventures we lived during those years in the Air Force!

When he opted to leave the military in 1974, we found ourselves back home in Idalou. Throughout the time spent in the military, Lee J. had helped me release more of the Alexandra side of my personality. Being away from home helped "her" emerge and subsequently blossom. I loved who I had become. When we returned home, I was a comfortable mixture of both Sandy and Alexandra. Yes, there were times when I had to deal with some of my high anxiety issues. Yes, I still had to deal with my innate bashful nature. You can't change your genetics, but you can learn to deal with them successfully. My biggest success in this realm is embedded in the story I'm about to share.

In 1978, all the kids were in school, and I knew we could use some extra money. Daddy and Dan were in need of a "secretary" at the Kirby store, and they offered me the job. So I went to work for them. They owned a very successful Kirby vacuum cleaner store in Lubbock. I soon learned to love my job, which would turn out to be far more than bookkeeping and being a receptionist. Initially, my anxiety was upped once more; I was trying something new. I had learned so much about myself during our military time that I was able to quickly adapt. Soon, I became both comfortable and competent in my role as the Kirby store's "secretary."

I watched how Daddy used his people skills to engage customers when they came in. Time after time, they would leave the store with a new Kirby vacuum cleaner being loaded into their cars. **He was really quite the salesman!** Over time, both Daddy and Dan started to leave the store with only me and our repairman. What do you know! I found that I could sell those Kirby's, too. I've said before that my anxiety had a genetic component to it that came from my daddy. Well, his salesmanship obviously had a genetic component, too, and it appeared he had passed it along to me.

At the start of 1981, I had been working at the Kirby store for about three years. We had built our house by then. Even before we got totally involved in building the house, I had a sense I (Alexandra) would like to have something that I could call my own in the business world. As I've said before, I loved my job at the Kirby store, and I had learned so much from Daddy. The shy little girl that was Sandy of old had been replaced with the business version of Alexandra. Alexandra could banter with the customers and make them feel at home. She could demonstrate a vacuum and then quite competently close the sale. I once told Lee J. that I knew how a football player who had just scored a touchdown felt. Every time I made a sale, I scored my touchdown, and I loved that feeling.

Any thoughts of stepping out and doing something else got pushed back while we were involved in building our house, but now all of that was completed. Some of the old feelings of looking outside of working for someone else at the Kirby store had returned. I knew my long-term future was not working for Daddy and Dan, but I had no clue what my future might be. Lee J. sensed my restlessness and suggested that we look for a business we could buy. I thought it couldn't hurt for him to start looking. So, he started watching the classified ads for "businesses for sale." Several months later, he saw something that we might want to check out—a small window covering shop for sale. As it turned out, when we checked into it, it was the shop where I had bought all the blinds for our new house the previous year. We started looking into it, and then the discussion began between Lee J.

and me. The thought of stepping into something so radically new allowed my old-time anxiety to raise its head once more. I told him, "I know nothing about the mini blind business."

He countered with, "You knew nothing about the Kirby vacuum cleaner business when you first started. Look how that turned out!"

I told him, "Borrowing money to buy a business is going to make me really nervous."

He laughed as he countered, "Sandy, everything makes you nervous at first, but I'm sure Alexandra will do just fine."

These conversations went on for a few days, and then, after seeing the store's books, it did look like something that would work for me after I learned the business a bit. I don't remember exactly what we paid the owner for it, but it was affordable, and we had no problem borrowing what we needed to get started.

In early 1981, we took ownership of The Window Gallery. We were now the proud new owners of our own small business. It was in a good location on the loop in southwest Lubbock at Indiana Avenue. The young girl (I don't remember her name.) who had worked with me when I ordered all the blinds for our house was still working for the previous owners. To abbreviate things, I'll call the previous owner MJ. MJ was going to "train" me and show me the ropes. Let me be frank about MJ. She was an arrogant, egotistical snob who treated me like her employee, not the new owner of the store. Let's just say Alexandra dismissed (fired?) her after about three days. Getting dismissed really pissed her off, but I was only returning to her the same type of behavior I was receiving from her.

Honestly, I was much smarter than she was. Quickly, I saw that there really wasn't much she was going to teach me. I had learned during the time we were in the Air Force to push aside any hesitancy caused by my anxiety and shyness and take charge of a situation when it was called for. MJ's firing was called for. (As I'm writing this section about the firing of MJ, I confess I have the biggest smirky grin on my face you can imagine.) The girl who had been MJ's employee did help me out for a few days, and she was very helpful, but soon I was on my own.

MJ and her husband had started the store from scratch three years earlier and had done pretty well. They had built a word-of-mouth customer base that made the business cash flow from the first day we owned it. I soon realized that there were a lot of other products that could be a part of the business, and I gradually looked for ways to expand what I sold. Those first months were great on-the-job training sessions for me. MJ had never tried to expand their service products much at all. I found one local workroom and another older lady who worked out of her home and could make custom drapes for me. It wasn't a great situation, but it was a start. I was making more money than I made as an hourly employee at the Kirby store, and I was learning the business. Alexandra was happy.

As the new year, 1982, began, a couple of things happened that would change everything. The first was that another space had opened up in the shopping center that was about four times as large as our current store. It was just two doors down. We approached our landlord about renting it. Lee J. made one of his bartering "deals" with him. He would do what remodeling was needed to the new space in return for a reduced rental rate. Our landlord went for it, and Lee J. went to work.

The advantage of the new space was that I now would have plenty of room to expand the number of samples I could carry. Plus, there was plenty of room to have some impressive displays. In a relatively short time, we moved two doors down. The store could now start to grow as I (Alexandra) was really finding my comfort zone since my confidence level in what I was doing was growing on a daily basis. For the first time ever, I was answerable to myself. I was truly my own boss. Subconsciously, I also was no longer constricted by my mother's mantras from my childhood. I had learned that I had unintentionally carried them with me even after I got married. I also no longer felt any of my self-inflicted pressure to please Daddy like I felt when I worked at the Kirby store. Alexandra was becoming a very independent and capable businesswoman, and she/I was loving it.

The other thing that was monumental to the success of the store was the fact that Wynona Westbrooke and I found each other. The story of how that happened is a bit unique. Julie wore one of my blazers to school one day. I had worn that blazer to work the previous day, and in the pocket of that blazer were several business cards. Julie found them and thought she would just give them out to some of the girls in the dressing room as they were getting dressed after PE. One of the girls who took a card was the daughter of Wynona Westbrooke. The girl gave her mother the card she had gotten from Julie, and Wynona called me that night. I had no idea that at her home in Idalou, she had a drapery workroom set up in a building in her backyard, and she was looking for work. A marriage from heaven was in the making.

She had learned her trade working as a workroom employee of the premier drapery store in Lubbock during the '60s and '70s. I would quickly learn that she was an artisan! I gave her a job to work on the next day, and her finished product was impeccable. I had stumbled into having my own contract workroom that catered to **me**. Wynona was a true artist in every sense of the word. She and I became very good friends. We were such an unlikely pair; she smoked like a freight train, and her speech was straight from redneck village. We did have to allow a couple of days for her finished product to air out a bit before we could hang it, but no one ever complained about a smoke smell.

Alexandra soon learned that she could bluff her way (if needed) with almost any customer because if the customer had a picture or sketch of it, **Wynona could make it.** Many times, as the years went by, Alexandra would tell a potential customer that we could do something that we had never tried before. I would tell the customer, "Oh sure, no problem with that!" Wynona never failed to always come through. Lee J. used to kid me that Wynona and I could design a $10,000 job with just a Big Chief tablet and a crayon. We probably could have.

Let me touch on some other aspects of the business I haven't mentioned yet. I didn't do a lot of advertising. The customer base I was developing was diverse, to say the least. The products I was learning to sell were going into upper middle-class homes and some of the high-end homes being built in Lubbock at that time. My customers were the wives of doctors, lawyers, academia from Texas Tech, well-to-do farmers, people from the oil patch, and assorted others. I think you get the idea. But it was word-of-mouth from someone in each of these types of groups that made my business thrive. Many of my customers, I could truly call friends. I, Alexandra, tried to keep the atmosphere in the store relaxed and welcoming. I learned about their families, jobs, husbands, and just whatever they wanted to talk about. Most sales were made after an appointment with them in their home. I always tried to go by and see the finished product after it was installed. I took great pride in providing customer satisfaction.

I must add that the area I served was huge. It was anything within a 120-mile radius of Lubbock. When I think back now, I traveled quite a large area of West Texas by myself; I then would go into a near stranger's home, again by myself. I'm amazed that I could do that. Those were the days before cell phones, so this formerly highly anxious and bashful woman really stepped out of what was once her comfort zone. To be able to do my job, I was out there alone and totally on my own and yet, I did my job quite well. By 1986, the store was doing three to four times the volume it was doing when we first bought it. I was extremely busy with the store, plus I had three daughters to see to. When we first bought the store, Julie was in high school, Angie was in junior high, and Marnie was in elementary school. My life was busy, to say the least, but I was loving it.

Initially, Lee J. handled the installations and learned to be very good at it. However, he likes to tell the story of how Alexandra fired him when she thought he had become "undependable." He loves to say it took two guys to replace him. One was a part-time Pentecostal preacher and his partner, an alcoholic who periodically didn't work on Mondays for being "sick" (hungover??). Anyway, after Willie and Boone became my regular installers, installations always went very well. In all fairness, the installation aspect of a sale had grown to the point where Lee J. could not satisfactorily handle them in a timely manner. He'd much rather say that Alexandra fired him rather than say that he quit. My "dear" husband likes to embellish things sometimes just to get a laugh, and his story of Alexandra firing him has consistently gotten him some laughs over the years.

I did have help from Julie and Angie when they were in college at times. Julie helped in 1983 and 1984. She and Robert got married in December of 1984. Robert was in the Navy, and she left with him to go to Norfolk, Virginia, where he was stationed. Angie worked with me at the store in the late '80s. She was exceptional, but she wanted to teach, and when she started her teaching career that ended her days at the store. When they kept the store, that would allow me to go on appointments during store hours, which was a big help. But most of the time, it was just me.

By 1985, I had subs who did everything from custom furniture upholstery, wallpaper, upholstered walls, and custom bedspreads—just about anything a person could want from a decorating shop. My primary business was still window treatments of all kinds, but the other things I just mentioned added to the versatility of the store.

Since I had several customers' wives whose husbands were lawyers, I got an interesting referral to do some decorating for one of the lawyer's clients. This client just happened to run an illegal bookmaking and gambling establishment in southwest Lubbock. They had an extra "entertainment room" in their facility that they wanted to spruce up a bit. They wanted a total blackout window treatment that was tasteful. When I went out to see what I was dealing with, I found a bedroom that had one wall with a window, one wall with a bed, and the other two walls only had mirrors on them. Also, the ceiling had a large mirror on it directly over the bed (Very interesting??). The only furniture was a king-sized bed with one nightstand. I was so naïve; I didn't really realize what those guys were doing in there until Lee J. explained it to me.

He also (kiddingly?) suggested maybe we should think about adding something like that to our bedroom. He told me he was sure he could do the work himself. **I told him that he** was an idiot. (Although, thinking back??? Hmmmm...oh well!) We did get the job. No credit cards; they dealt only in cash, no receipt required. I only tell this story to show how diverse my customer base was. The fact that someone, my husband, had to explain to me what was going on there shows that I was still somewhat of an innocent country girl with a lot to learn about the world. But, oh, how much I had learned about myself!

Previously, I talked about how, early on, I was always in Lee J.'s shadow, and I was fine with that. However, the purchase of The Window Gallery was for **me.** It became "my baby." I guess originally, we thought we were going to be equal participants in the business, but it soon became apparent to both Lee J. and me that **I was The Window Gallery.** Most people didn't even know who the guy was that hung around in the back of the store from time to time. After Alexandra fired him as her installer, he really wasn't around all that much. He did continue to do the books for the store, however. This was a total role reversal for us. I was not Lee J.'s wife so much as he was Sandy's (Alexandra's) husband. No one called or asked to speak to him. No one asked him to give them an estimate. Essentially, no one asked him about anything to do with the store. He used to kid me that I'd have to promote him to just be the store's official flunky. The beauty of this was that Lee J. was just fine with it all. He was so proud of me, and so was Daddy.

I'll pick up the story back from the front porch of my folks' house that Sunday when Daddy told Lee J. and Dan, **"That**

Sandy is something, isn't she?" Lee J. readily agreed. (He better have!) He told me later that it was apparent from their discussion that day that Daddy knew that my choice of foregoing college to get married was the right choice for me and that he now completely accepted it. It took a while for Daddy to get over his disappointment that I wasn't going to attend college, but over time, he gradually realized that college was not for everyone. He watched me grow as a competent salesperson when I worked at the Kirby store. Then, he watched me become a very successful business owner at The Window Gallery. For some reason, just before that Sunday, he found out just how successful our little business venture had become. Mother said he was about to "bust his buttons" over how proud he was of his "favorite" daughter. (I say "favorite" here tongue-in-cheek.)

How successful was our little business venture back then? Since Lee J. was the bookkeeper, he recalls that in the late eighties, I was netting over $250,000 per year in today's dollars. One more takeaway from my years of running the store: that shy, anxious, hesitant Sandy of old was no more. The Alexandra part of me was at the forefront when it came to the business, though Sandy was still there for the family, especially those sweet grandchildren. (Well, maybe some of the boys weren't all that sweet.) I ended my years in retail sales a few years later as a competent businesswoman with self-esteem and self-confidence to spare. I liked what I had accomplished; I had proven my point to Daddy and myself. For me, college was not a necessity; when the time came, I was satisfied to take a slower track and just be proud that it had been a great run. I was content with that.

I have one more thought to add. My mother would probably turn over in her grave to read these last few pages. For years, I lived under her mantra that one should "never tooteth thine own horn." Well, I confess, in these previous pages, "I **tooted,** and it wasn't me passing gas."

Pretty as a Picture, Tough as a Boot

Sitting in a darkened movie theater, my thoughts were, *Why am I here because this is not fun.* I was sitting next to my "boyfriend," Gary, who I really had decided I didn't even like, and here I was on a "date" with him. Earlier, his mother had dropped us off at the theater. We were both in the eighth grade and fourteen years old. The strangest thing about all this was that his mother had chosen me as his girlfriend. Somehow, I had gotten left out of the choosing process. I hardly remember ever talking to Gary much at all. As the movie went on, I was paying no attention to it; I was totally lost in a jumble of thoughts, one of which was, *How did I ever let myself get in this situation?* At that moment, I had no answer.

Finally, the movie was over. We once more got in the car and his mother dropped me off at my house. It was over! It had been awkward; it had been anxiety-inducing; it had been downright painful. As I write these words and ponder about why I found myself in such a miserable situation, the only thing I could come up with was that I accepted Gary's invitation because I didn't want to be impolite. (Looking back, that was beyond stupidity!) Politeness or not, I decided that I would not put myself in another situation with him like that again.

The event just described was the last time I had one of those "dates" with Gary. Initially, I had kind of liked him, but as time went on, I found that I definitely didn't like him as a boyfriend at all. I think the fact that I had such a close relationship with Barb and Brenda was a factor in my feelings not only for Gary but for all the boys my age in my class. As I spent more and more time with my sisters and their friends, a stark contrast in the maturity of the boys their age and the boys of my age became apparent. My mental maturity was far outpacing my actual age. When it came to my interest in the opposite sex, I was a very conflicted young teenage girl. This would resolve itself during the summer after my eighth-grade year. But first, let me explain some things about my two years in junior high school.

As I've said earlier, I had never enjoyed school throughout my years in elementary school. I made top notch grades, and I knew I was the smartest kid in my class. My grades bore evidence of that. I knew I was considered the prettiest girl in my class. (I'll use the word "considered" here because if I said I **was** the prettiest girl, then I would violate Mother's rule about tooting your own horn.) I'm sure that my looks and the fact that I tried to be nice to everyone were the reasons Gary's mom chose me to be her son's girlfriend. That put me in the position of being asked to go on those "dates" with him. After the last one I just described, I made the decision that I wasn't going to put myself in that position again. I was growing up.

In the fall of 1959, I entered the seventh grade and began two years of junior high school. My last years in elementary school had started to toughen me up. By that, I mean I could push my feelings and emotions down and get through situations that my overanxiousness and shyness made very difficult for me. The subjects where I didn't generally have to get up in front of the class to give a report of some kind were the ones I liked, but subjects like English or social studies that sometimes required speaking in front of the class were another story. Something as simple as giving a book report in an English class was a major thing for me early on. By the time sixth grade rolled around, I could get through things like that and not show any outward signs of my inner turmoil. I think my mother's "get over it" attitude was always in the background. It gave me an added determination to do what was required without showing my inner feelings. The fact that my reports were generally flawless helped, too.

The seventh grade was when organized athletics in school began and I found I liked to play basketball. Having two older sisters to play ball with at home obviously had helped in improving my skills, and having Daddy as my coach didn't hurt either. He was always an encourager. I was an above-average player, and I really enjoyed the practices, but the games were a different story. Having an audience in the stands took away most of the "fun" part for me. Again, I just suppressed what I was feeling and played the best I could. However, for me, the practices were where the fun was.

I know this may sound strange, but despite my anxiety and bashfulness, I wanted to be a cheerleader. I tried out and was elected in both my seventh and eighth-grade years. I think I discovered that being a part of a group activity like cheerleading did not make me the center of attention. It was obvious that I was a conflicted young teenager and after the experience of raising three daughters of my own, I think all teenage girls live with at least some inner conflict during that stage of their lives. There was the part of me that liked the attention a cheerleader generated and another part of me that had to deal with my shyness and anxiety. I can see now that it was during this part of my life that I started learning some life lessons that would serve me well in later years. I was learning that if I wanted something, sometimes the only way for me to be successful was to work hard and push through whatever the obstacle might be. In my case, pushing through my obstacles of shyness and anxiety was more of suppressing and hiding them rather than actually pushing through them. Either way, I was learning to cope.

As my eighth-grade year was winding down, cheerleader tryouts for the next year were coming up and I wanted to be a cheerleader again. However, this time, I would be in front of the entire high school, and my anxiety was off the charts. It also was to be the first time I became aware that I was attracting the attention of older boys. During these tryouts for the single freshman cheerleader slot, Lee J. remembers that when I came out on the gym floor, the older boys in the stands went completely overboard in their vocal reception of me. There were a lot of whistles, whoops, and such. He says that he was a part of the raucous group of boys that had such a reaction to me that day.

I personally don't remember anything about the reaction I got. It was probably because my anxiety was through the roof, and I was strictly focused on getting through my tryout routine. What I do remember is that upon completion of my routine, I ran off the court and breathed a gigantic sigh of relief. I had done it; it was over! I think that up to that point in my life, that tryout was the hardest thing I'd ever done in front of a crowd. Once again, I had toughened up and steeled my way through it. When the votes were counted, I had won the spot for the freshman cheerleader on the five-girl squad. I was happy that I had won, but it also left me quite anxious.

At the very end of school that spring, there was one other thing that pushed me to the limit of what I was capable of doing—giving the valedictory speech for my eighth-grade graduation exercise. I think giving that speech was even more difficult for me to do than the cheerleader tryout. This time, I was to speak in front of both my peers and adults. I was very competitive when it came to my grades. I did my homework; I listened in class; I studied for my tests. I wanted to be first in my class even though I knew it entailed giving a speech in front of a big audience at the end of the year. I think the fact that the audience was made up of both my classmates and their parents made this a really difficult thing for me to do. The time came; I wrote my speech, and I gave it. Unlike being on the field as a cheerleader or a member of the basketball team, I was up there at the podium all alone. All eyes were on me, but I came through. It was a good lesson for me that I could do things that seemed impossible.

Looking back with a much clearer view of myself, I realize I really wanted to be popular, and I clearly succeeded. In the eighth grade, I was chosen to be the football sweetheart, elected queen for the athletic banquet, and was the eighth-grade girl class favorite. I evidently wanted the reward enough to get through my bashfulness and anxiety. I realize now that I had gotten through many, many situations with no help from anyone. I had figured it all out on my own. I somehow developed coping mechanisms that seemed to work for me. Again, it was something I did strictly on my own. I think the psychological definition of what I used to cope with my inner struggles was physical withdrawal from uncomfortable circumstances coupled with emotional suppression of my feelings and emotions.

Soon, school was out and the summer of 1961 began. It was to be what both Lee J. and Barb have called the summer when my overall maturity went into overdrive. Physically, Lee J. says my feminine attributes "blossomed." I would have to agree; it was the time when, he laughingly says, I became a "fully-growed" young woman, though I was only fourteen years old. Barb says that I could have easily passed as a senior rather than a freshman. Either way, I liked what I had become. I also liked the attention I was getting, even though I was still painfully shy.

My mental maturity also took a big leap. I was completely comfortable being with my older sisters and their friends. Although, due to my shyness, I was mostly a spectator rather than a participant when I was with them. During that summer, Barb and Brenda invited me to join them when they would make the "drag" in Idalou. Lee J. says he first noticed me then and began to think about asking me for a date.

Lee J. had a slight problem, though. My sisters' boyfriends were brothers and they had a friend named Milton who hung around with them a lot. (He was a classmate of Lee J.) I found myself thrust into a situation where I was kind of expected to "be with" their friend, Milton. He was a nice enough guy, but I had absolutely no interest in him whatsoever as someone I would ever want to date. I finally had to tell Barb to not put me in any more situations where I would "be with" Milton. She immediately made sure that didn't happen anymore, and it didn't; she was a good big sister.

I knew who Lee J. was, but I'd never really taken any notice of him since he was three years older than me. I found out later that Barb and Brenda were giving him hints to think about asking me out. Finally, in late August, he called and asked me for a date. My life was about to change forever.

Being wired to avoid confrontational situations and suppressing my emotions had worked fine for me as a young girl in elementary and junior high schools, but it had left me with a lot of emotional baggage that I would take with me into adulthood. A time would come when I would start to feel that something inside me was yearning to find a release. I'm so thankful that the guy I was about to fall in love with and who would eventually become my husband would one day have a part in helping me find release from much of what I was holding inside. A part of what I was holding inside was a whole new persona that I had no idea even existed within me. What memories I have of those times when all these things started finding a release!

KISSES SWEETER THAN WINE

It was the sixth week of school during my freshman year in high school, and I found myself in the first makeout session of my life. This was our seventh date since Lee J. had first asked me out just before school started earlier that August. Because it was so memorable for me, I looked up a 1961 calendar online and figured out that what I'm describing occurred on Friday, October 6, 1961. It was an unusual Friday night date for us because it was the open week of football season for Idalou that year.

Since he wasn't playing football that night, and I wasn't cheering, we had decided to stay around my house instead of going anywhere. We had staked out the couch in our dining area while Barb and Dan were on the couch around the corner in our living room. They were engaged to be married the next spring, and they were looking for some private time themselves. The rest of the family was back in their own rooms, so there was no one around but the four of us. They couldn't see us, and we couldn't see them. Lee J. had peeked around the corner; they were also involved in a "close encounter" of their own.

What I was experiencing that night was all new to me. Seven weeks earlier, on our first date, Lee J. had kissed me goodnight quite passionately and I was not prepared for a kiss like that. I was just fourteen years old and had never experienced anything like the kiss he gave me. Yet here I was seven weeks later, enjoying myself like never before. My mind and body had never felt anything like what was going on inside me. We were both exploring a world together that I had no experience in at all. Lee J. told me later that he'd had a little prior experience once before, but he said it was nothing like what we felt that night. This was to be the beginning of a passion between the two of us that has lasted over 63 years as of this writing. Let me take you back to that first date with my future husband just a few weeks earlier.

Lee J. had finally gotten up his courage to call and ask me for a date to go to the finale of Idalou's fiftieth-anniversary celebration. Of course, I had to ask Mother for permission, and she agreed to let me go. After reading the past chapters, I'm sure some would think it strange that I would be allowed to go on a date with a boy three years older than me. Lee J. wasn't sure if Mother would let me go out with him either. However, my folks knew his folks; we went to church together, he was considered to be a good Baptist boy, etc. Therefore, I was allowed to go to this close-by local event with him. We really had never had a chance to talk and get to know one another. I was always with my older sisters and, being who she was, Barb did most of the talking.

Lee J. showed up on time, and Barb answered the door. She called me and announced that he had arrived. I had no idea at the time that I would make such an impression on him that night. The following is a direct quote from his words taken from his autobiography.

"*As she walked into the living room, there before me stood the most beautiful girl I had ever seen. She had on a red and white top along with a pair of white fitted shorts all made by her mother. Her outfit left no doubt that she was a dazzlingly beautiful young girl; I was completely blown away. I guess I had never really seen her up so close and personal. She was just plain gorgeous! As I look back now, that was one of those 'take my breath away' moments.*"

It's a good thing that I didn't realize the impression I'd made on him at the time. As usual, my anxiety was really ramped up. He walked me to the car, and we left on the short drive to downtown Idalou for the festivities we were to attend. I guess we were both nervous, because I don't remember anything about our conversation until the program was over and a square dance began. There were some other kids around, and we both talked to them for a while, then we talked with each other. He really seemed nice, and I relaxed a bit. Neither of us knew anything about how to square dance (being non-dancing Baptists and all), so we just hung around for a while, and then he took me home.

Just before we were going to get out of the car, he turned toward me and kissed me. **I mean, he really kissed me!** It was a surprise for which I was not prepared. I'm sure my surprise showed on my face, but somehow, he walked me to the door, and I went in. He would tell me later that he knew immediately that the kiss had been a big mistake. He wondered if I would go out with him again since he had been so forward. Of course, Barb and Brenda had to get the date report from me, but I didn't tell them about the kiss. I just said

I had a really good time.

School started the next week, and, of course, we saw each other there. We had a chance to talk some more, and he asked if I would like to go to the "show" with him the next Saturday night. Again, I told him I would have to ask my mother, and I would let him know the next day. Again, she gave me her permission, and our habit of a weekly movie date on Saturday nights began. My shyness and anxiety were quickly starting to fall away as I saw him periodically the rest of the week at school.

Our date that week and the one the next week were great. We were getting acquainted and starting to really like each other's company. The only thing about our second and third date was that he did not kiss me either time. I was beginning to get worried. The more I thought about that first date kiss, the more I wanted to try it again. It would be our fourth date before he would kiss me goodnight again. That time, his kiss was soft; it was tender; it was sensuous; and it was **wonderful.** I can still feel the thrill of that kiss even today. I was losing my heart to this guy at the ripe age of fourteen. I know that some who read this would say what I was feeling could not have been real. But you have to believe me when I say what I felt then is the same thing I feel now sixty-three years later each time he kisses me. Things that are not real don't have a life expectancy of sixty-three years.

I've named this chapter after the title of a song by Anita Bryant. It was a big hit back in the late fifties, and the song tells a story very similar to my life. Of course, kissing is the first very personal thing that a couple does in the beginning of a relationship. They say that kissing releases a lot of "feel good" chemicals in our brains. Those chemicals were working overtime for me that Friday night in October. That night, making out with Lee J. was the first time I began to feel that he was the one I wanted to spend my life with. It seems to have worked out.

As the year wore on, I found that being with him tended to wipe away a lot of my anxiety. Oh, I could still get anxious about school stuff, but the anxiousness I once felt as an elementary school kid about anything and everything was diminishing. My shyness was not nearly as intense as it once was. I think my being a cheerleader was also helping in that regard. Rita Bartlett was one of the senior cheerleaders, and she took me under her wing. I relaxed and actually started enjoying being in front of a crowd at the football games. I probably was as happy as I'd ever been since I had started school nine years earlier.

When my birthday neared in November, Lee J. wanted to get me something really special. He asked Brenda if she would meet him in Lubbock to try on some clothes that she thought I might like. We wore the same size back then. He and Brenda found a beautiful light blue skirt and sweater set that he bought for me. He gave it to me for my birthday, and I loved it. However, Mother thought it was too expensive and thought I should give it back. She finally relented and let me keep it.

The only thing that turned out to be a downer that fall, happened after football season was over. It was an incident at one of my basketball games. I had told Lee J. that I didn't want him to attend any of my games because, with him in the stands, my anxiety would go off the charts. He was clueless about how my anxiety affected me. I had become quite adept at hiding it, even from him. The season had started some time earlier, and for some reason, he sneaked into one of my games and tried to hide in the corner. Well, I saw him and he knew I'd seen him. After the game, I was so mad at him. He apologized repeatedly, and of course, I accepted his apology, but I made the decision to quit basketball strictly because of my anxiety issues. I was almost to the point of calling it quits before the incident with Lee J., but he was the straw that broke the camel's back. I turned in my uniform the next day.

By now, Lee J. and I had been dating for a little over three months. Mother had given me an eleven pm curfew, and there would also be no sitting in the car in front of the house after getting home from a date. (We wouldn't want the neighbors to talk, would we?) However, Dan was seeing Barb a lot, and they were generally there on the nights when we had a date. Mother made sure that they had some private time, and of course, we got to take advantage of that, too. I had turned fifteen in November so I didn't think I seemed quite so young anymore. I have to be honest, I loved being close to Lee J. and I really loved him kissing me. I couldn't seem to get enough. Our kissing elicited feelings in me that I had never known before. They were both mental and physical. I was getting quite an education when I was with him. One of the things that I liked the most was that my anxiety issues became temporarily nonexistent. Just being with him made me feel relaxed; made me feel warm; made me feel safe; **made me feel**

special. It was becoming a wonderful time for me each time we were together. My thoughts after each date would soon turn to anticipation of the next time I would see him.

We saw each other daily at school, and he would generally take me home after school when football season ended. I was happy, and he seemed happy too. We were becoming a typical high school teenage couple. It was something very common for the times. This was about the time I got chastened by my mother for being too "familiar" with Lee J. at the basketball games. When I told Lee J. what she had said, he wasn't sure what we were doing that Mother thought was inappropriate. It actually made me more than a little angry, but as usual, I didn't argue and **suppressed** my anger. I'm not sure we did anything differently, but she never said anything along those lines again. It was just another reminder of the always-present pressure that I felt from my mother and her rules. I suppose we quit holding hands or something that had to have been quite innocuous.

As the school year went on, we spent as much time together as possible. After Barb and Dan got married in the spring, Mother still left us alone and made sure we had the hour between eleven pm and midnight pretty much to ourselves. We certainly took advantage of that time. By the time school was out for the summer, I think we both knew that we were destined to spend our lives together.

Daddy's summer job was measuring crops for the USDA, and he helped Lee J. get the same job. It was the first real job Lee J. had ever had, and he loved it. For the first time in his life, he had his own money. It was also the time that he got the 1959 Pontiac that we both grew to love. It was such a beautiful car. He needed it for his summer job, but he also needed it to go back and forth to Texas Tech when he started college in the fall. I will say that measuring crops for the summer let Lee J. become very familiar with the farms in northeast Lubbock County.

To be quite honest, by this time, we were a normal young couple, and we both wanted to be alone more and more. Lee J. was conflicted about our mounting desires, **but I was not.** He truly was trying to respect the edicts that he had been taught from all his years of being in church. We were nowhere near the stage of having sex, but we both wanted some real alone time. That summer he found the perfect place where that could happen. Needless to say, we had some great makeout sessions that we both loved. As I mentioned earlier, the title of this chapter came from the title of a popular song from that era. The lyrics say it all for me.

> *When I was a young girl and never been kissed*
> *I got to thinkin' it over how much I had missed*
> *So I got me a guy and kissed him and then*
> *Oh Lord well I kissed him again*
>
> *Because he had kisses sweeter than wine*
> *He had mm-mm kisses sweeter than wine*
>
> (*Kisses Sweeter Than Wine*, sung by Anita Bryant)

When I initially listened to the recording of that old song, my thoughts were that I certainly identified with the intimate theme of that song. **Lee J. was and still is one sweet kisser.**

During that summer, there was a slow, incremental

increase in our desire for closeness. I think that my long-held suppressed emotions contributed to the intensity of what I was feeling. I didn't know exactly what was stirring in me just under the surface. I had never been outwardly rebellious toward anything my mother might disapprove of, but something within me now had a rebellious feel about it when it came to the way I was feeling toward Lee J.

As that summer came to an end, I found that the past year had been the happiest year I could ever remember. Lee J. and I had found each other, and our relationship had blossomed into what we both knew was true love. He was going to live at home for his first year of college, and I would go on to high school for my sophomore year. I would soon find that high school without Lee J. was nothing like the year before, even though we continued to see each other several times a week. It was nothing like the year before when I saw him every day at school. During that summer, he tried to make a stop at our house before he headed home after he'd finished his day measuring the crops. It was a good summer, and our love would continue to grow.

YOUNG LOVE

(The Best of Times, the Worst of Times)

Lee J. and I had just parked in our usual place where we could really be alone for a while before we would go home to meet my eleven pm curfew. It was in December, just a few days before Christmas, during my sophomore year in high school. We had been dating for well over a year. We were both sure that someday we would get married and spend the rest of our lives together. I was sixteen and Lee J. was eighteen. (We were pretty young for such an elaborate plan. Huh?)

Our love and passion for each other had continued to grow, and in recent days, we were consistently getting into heavy petting sessions each time we found ourselves parked there. A part of me had been awakened that was yearning for more, much more. Lee J. had some of the same feelings, but due to his upbringing, he was conflicted. For some reason, I was not. We both had grown up being taught the doctrines of the Baptist Church; premarital sex was unequivocally forbidden in the teachings we had heard all our lives. But here we were, two teenagers desperately in love with each other with no chance of getting married for another year and a half.

We both knew of too many couples over the years who found themselves in a situation similar to ours, and the girl got pregnant. Most ended up getting married, but it was never an ideal situation. Scandal enveloped the families;

education was cut short; sometimes animosities between the families developed. Neither Lee J. nor I wanted to find ourselves in such a situation. As we held each other there that night, instead of our usual stoking the fire of our smoldering passions, we talked.

It was obvious that Lee J. had been thinking a lot about the path we both knew we were on. I don't remember the exact conversation we had, but I do remember as we talked, he asked me a couple of questions. One was, "If we had a piece of paper that said we were married and it was okay for us to have sex, would it change anything about the way you feel about me? Would it change the commitment you have to me?"

I answered with an emphatic, "No!"

Then he said, "Me neither!" (Whoa! That's quite a conversation for two teenagers to have sitting in a darkened parked car on an isolated turnrow.) As we embraced each other, we both vowed that what we had was forever. Neither of us knew what the future held for us, but whatever it was, it would be the two of us together, and **it has been!**

I know some who read my words will think that I was simply an immature teenager who "thought" she was in love. If that's what it was, I'll take my immature teenage utterances over some grandiose vows I've heard exchanged at more than one wedding where I've been in attendance. A couple of those marriages lasted less than two years, ours just went over **sixty.**

That night, together, we made a conscious decision that soon we would consummate our relationship. I think that was the night I coined the phrase, "we just can't not do it!" We realized that was the way we both felt. When I said it, Lee J. just smiled and agreed. The Christmas holidays and New Year's celebrations precluded us from acting on our desires very quickly. The one thing that we promised each other was that we would be careful.

Of course, in those days, it generally fell upon the boy to take care of the contraception. It would be in early January when we both lost our virginity to each other. Thinking back about our first time, neither one of us knew quite what to do, we were awkward, yet Lee J. was so tender with me. He was concerned not to hurt me. He didn't. Though the act itself didn't last very long, I thought it was wonderful. Whether I was or not, I felt like a real woman.

And so began a year and a half of intense sexual activity between us that we kept entirely private. I'm not aware that anyone ever suspected what was going on between us. In retrospect, this probably should have been a time of great emotional stress for me. I was hiding something enormous, and yet I felt a calmness and absolutely no anxiety whatsoever about our clandestine activities. I would occasionally have some anxiety about something going on at school, but I had no anxiety about the private activities Lee J. and I were having. I loved all the other times we were enjoying just being together at our house, going to school activities, going to movies, and such. We simply loved each other's company. We had not only become lovers but best friends.

As I previously mentioned, the previous summer, Daddy had helped Lee J. get a job measuring crops for the USDA office in Lubbock. It was a perfect job for him! I suppose Daddy had figured out that he was probably going to be a permanent fixture in the family. Lee J. was very successful in the job and would work there again the following summer. I know he really appreciated what Daddy did for him in getting that job. It was the first time he'd ever had what he called a real job with a salary.

We saw each other quite regularly that summer and enjoyed doing a lot of the normal outdoor activities that others our age were involved in. I think the fact that our relationship had grown into something that made me a part of something bigger than myself allowed me to relax and just enjoy the times we were together during those months. I'd found that he was someone I could confide in and tell him anything with no fear of judgment or disapproval. That was so different for me, and the way I felt being a part of my family. I loved all my family, but I'd never felt free to confide in any of them like I could with Lee J. Our relationship now made everything different for me. I found I wanted to be with him all the time. Of course, I knew that wasn't possible. It was always a downer for me having to say goodnight and him having to leave (the worst of times).

I spent a lot of time in a bathing suit with Barb and Brenda that summer, getting a tan in our backyard. I knew Lee J. really liked the way I looked. It was sometime during that summer when he told me, "You are the prettiest girl I've ever seen."

When I asked him, "Why have you never told me that before?"

He was shocked and said, "I just thought you knew it."

As smart as he was/is, that was really dumb! I guess if you date a guy who has no feminine influences in his home life and therefore has no feminine mentor such as a sister, they can be really stupid when it comes to telling a girl what you really think. Like most teenage girls, I had some self-image issues. Little did he know that a compliment from him saying that I was the "prettiest girl he had ever seen" would have been priceless for me. Oh, well! He certainly corrected that mistake countless times in later years.

Too soon, our first summer together was over, and a new world for me began. In the fall of 1962, I was a high school sophomore, and Lee J. was a freshman at Tech. We still saw each other a lot, but I really hated school. I had a couple of girlfriends that I enjoyed being with, but most of the rest of my classmates, especially some of the boys, were just so immature. I didn't enjoy being around them at all. I was enduring school and hated being there. Yet my grades were still top of the class, and I planned on keeping them there. However, my thoughts were constantly on the next time Lee J. and I would see each other. I know that probably sounds somewhat weird, but that was just the way it was.

It was relatively early during my sophomore year that an idea began to take shape in my mind. As I related in a previous chapter, I had convinced Mother and Daddy to let me graduate from high school in three years instead of the usual four. I didn't think I could wait three more years before I could get married. It would only be two if I graduated early. So, I had to officially set up my graduation plan with Mr. Vaughn. I got that done sometime in November that year.

I should add here that though we were starting to plan for our wedding, Lee J. never officially proposed to me. It was kind of an evolutionary thing. At some point, we both realized that someday we would get married. I look back now and know that no proposal was more than a little unusual, but that's really the way it happened. I don't remember thinking it was strange at the time. It was during this time that Lee J. and I began discussing a general date for when we thought we could plan a wedding. We talked about the kind of family we would like to have. The subjects varied, but general planning for us as a married couple was beginning to happen. This all occurred sometime during the fall of my sophomore year in 1962.

I've talked about how we saw each other on a very regular basis but not much about our personal interactions at this time in our relationship. We could talk for hours about anything and everything. By this time, we had been dating for well over a year, and I knew 100% that he was the person I wanted to spend the rest of my life with.

I opened this chapter by telling the story of the night we made the conscious decision to become intimate with each other. Let me expand on that subject somewhat.

If you have sensed that everything I was doing to get out of school early was to enable us to get married as soon as possible, you would be correct. I'm sure someone from the younger generations reading this might ask, "Why the rush?" Here's the situation we faced. In the '60s, unlike the world of today, premarital sex was considered heinously wrong by almost everyone. It was highly condemned at church and those who did sin in such a way were going to spend eternity in Hell. Society and parents condemned it. But the reality was that there was still a lot of premarital sex going on.

As for us, I certainly didn't want to get pregnant before we got married, but it seems that in today's world, young couples move in together and think little about it. Easy access to contraception is available. Little stigma, if any, is attached to premarital sex. Well, let me tell you, **NONE** of that was available to Lee J. and me sixty years ago. Yet our passion for each other was off the charts! We still had to adhere to my mother's eleven pm curfew, and so we did. We were careful. He took proper precautions so that we didn't end up like some in our day and "have to get married." We both have been exclusive to each other for all these years and even today, our sexual passion for each other still runs high. Lee J. struggled with some "preacher-induced guilt," as he called it, for some time, but he finally came to terms with it. However, I never felt one iota of guilt about not being a virgin on my wedding night.

We continued to attend various school functions together when we could, and most of the time, they were fun. In the spring of 1963, I started planning to attend summer school at Lubbock High to gain the additional credits I would need for my early graduation. It was also going to require some correspondence courses, which I ordered and began working on. I was busy, but I was happy that things seemed to be working out. Being busy did seem to make the time go faster. We continued to see each other several times a week, and our relationship continued to strengthen.

When the next summer rolled around, Lee J. again worked at the ASCS office as he had done the year before, and I started summer school at Lubbock High. I went all summer and got two additional credits completed toward my high school graduation requirements. About this time, his dad had bought a boat, and we began going to Buffalo Lakes from time to time. His brother, Tootie, and his girlfriend, Ann, went with us a lot, and those were fun times. By the end of the summer, I think I began to realize that we only had to wait one more year before we could marry. My dreams were starting to come true.

That fall, Lee J. moved into the dorm for his sophomore year at Tech. It made his schedule easier to handle since his major had so many afternoon labs, but it certainly didn't stop him from making the twenty-minute drive to my house from the campus on a very regular basis. He said that the school year in the dorm gave him a little better perspective about the much bigger world that existed away from Lubbock and Idalou.

Sometime during the fall of my junior/senior year of high school, Lee J. and I thought it was about time that we asked our parents for their blessings on our marriage plans. I remember him coming over to our house and asking to speak to Mother and Daddy. He mustered up his courage, told them of our plans, and asked for their permission and blessings. Mother just grinned, as did Daddy, who said, of course, we had their blessing. He then said something to the effect that our plans for getting married had hardly been much of a secret in the Bramlett household for quite some time. We told them we planned to get engaged during the upcoming Christmas break, which was fine with them.

We then went out to Lee J.'s house to talk to his folks. We got a very similar reaction from his mom and dad. His daddy asked me about my plans. I told him I was going to get a job after graduation and that I was not interested in going on to school. I told him I just had no interest in a college degree. He then said they would pay for our apartment and all of Lee J.'s school expenses. I realized that was going to be a huge help. His mother seemed happy, too. She had long ago given up on the problem of our getting too serious.

The next week, we went ring shopping in Lubbock. I picked out this beautiful marquee set, and Lee J. bought it. We picked out a silver ring for him, and I bought it. Our official announcement was to be at Christmas. We were both excited. It seemed like the long wait would end next summer. During the Christmas break, we made it official by telling everyone what they already knew: our plan was to get married the next summer. I started wearing what I thought was the most beautiful engagement ring I had ever seen. Being engaged and finally wearing a ring was the most exciting thing that had ever happened to me in my life. Lee J. seemed equally excited, too; at least, he said so.

So, I went back to school for my final semester. The word was out that I would graduate in May, but I now officially belonged to no class. I was neither a junior nor a senior. It was somewhat surreal. I felt like a person in "no-man's land." But there was one thing that really stuck out that I remember quite clearly. I was informed by more than one girl in the senior class that I could not go on their senior trip. First off, the last thing I wanted to do was to go on anybody's senior trip, but I was a bit taken aback by the tackiness with which I was informed that I couldn't go. In fact, I later found out that they had a special class meeting to officially vote to say I couldn't go. They could have saved themselves a lot of trouble if anyone had bothered to just ask me if I wanted to go. My quick answer of "No" would have saved them some of the drama that ensued.

Graduation time neared, but I had not heard from my final correspondence course about my grade. I don't remember what the problem was, but Mr. Vaughn said it was fine for me to walk the stage, though my diploma would be unsigned. He would sign it after receiving my final grade. It came a few days later, and my diploma was signed. It was now official; I was a high school graduate. As it turned out, my final grades would have made me the valedictorian of the class of 1964 or my original class of 1965. Actually, I had the satisfaction of knowing that fact and also the relief of not having to give a valedictory address for either. That was a big win for my continuing anxiety issues.

After graduation, I got a job at Interstate Securities, and the work environment there soon deteriorated. I had a wedding to plan, so I got through it. I'll fill in the details in a later chapter. However, for the three months before our wedding, I worked there and still lived at home. I was still under Mother's tutelage. We were planning the wedding, and Mother was making all the dresses. Anticipation was in the air, and I was excited! However, there was one incident that reminded me of the pressure I still felt to adhere to Mother's rules.

I wanted a new bathing suit for our honeymoon. Two-piece bathing suits were in style, but I knew that would not be my mother's choice. For the first time ever, I felt something inside me just beneath the surface, and this time I wanted to please **me**. I wanted to do something maybe a little naughty or maybe slightly rebellious. I think Lee J. went with me to look at the bathing suit and even bought it for me. It was a **two-piece (Gasp!)**, and it exposed about twelve inches of my midriff. I brought it home to show Mother, and I did not get an approving look. However, she said nothing! Because I'd bought it for my honeymoon, I think she understood. I spent as much time as I could on the weekends to get a tan before the wedding, and this time, my tan included a twelve-inch part of me that had never seen the sun before. I loved it!

I subtitled this chapter, *The Best of Times, The Worst of Times*, because I knew shortly after we started dating that I had found the guy with whom I wanted to live my life, and the times we were together were the best. I always looked forward to the next time we would see each other. The worst was being locked into circumstances that precluded us from getting married for three years. I hated the waiting, but it turned out to be worth it many times over. Keeping our intimate activities hidden did not give me any anxiety issues of which I was consciously aware. But I would be fooling myself if I didn't admit that somewhere deep down, I had to have suppressed some feelings concerning this issue. I think, by this time in my life, I had become so adept at concealing such feelings that I didn't even recognize them myself. There was a lot inside me that someday I would eventually begin to release. Stay tuned.

FREEDOM

It was early, but the Sun was up and shining brightly. Light was pouring into our suite from the other room. We were lying in bed. This had been our first night in the honeymoon suite at the Jack Tar Hotel in Galveston, Texas. It had been a wonderful night. Though we had been intimate for over a year and a half, we had never gotten to make love in such an environment as this honeymoon suite. I lay there next to my new husband, again, our bare bodies snuggled closely together. I could tell he was awake. Then he rolled over, kissed me, and said, "Good morning."

I said, "Good morning to you, too."

I had never been this happy in my life. I'd never felt such freedom. I was free to touch, kiss, hold, embrace, but most of all, to give my whole being completely to this guy who was now my husband. Earlier, as I lay next to him, I cried silently, but my tears weren't sad tears; they were tears of joy like I'd never known before.

Suddenly, he broke the mood when he said, "Do you realize that I've never seen you totally naked in the daylight."

It kind of caught me off guard, but I thought about it and teased him with my own question, "Is that a request?"

Without hesitation, he said, "Well, it could be."

My thought was that this could be fun, so I said, "Close your eyes, let me get up, and I'll be right back."

He closed his eyes, I got up and went into the sitting room of the suite where the bathroom was located. I brushed out my hair a little, put on a little blush, and touched up my body with some powder. To be honest, shy little ol' me felt more than a little naughty, and I wanted to tease him. I told him from the other room, "Close your eyes and don't open them until I tell you to."

I peeked a little, and I could see that he was sitting up in the bed with his eyes closed. I moved to the doorway to the bedroom and stood there in as provocative a pose as I could muster. I was wearing nothing but a smile. (Well, it was more of a seductive smirk, I think.) Then I told him, "You can open your eyes now!"

I knew that the light behind me was providing a shadowing effect on my body. The bedroom was still darkened somewhat, but I knew he was going to get an eyeful. As he opened his eyes, the expression on his face was priceless. I learned right there that God had given us girls a mighty power when it comes to having a visual effect on our guys. He looked stunned for a moment, and then he said, "OH MY GOD, YOU-ARE-SO-BEAUTIFUL."

He slowly got up and started toward me. It was evident that I'd had quite an effect on him. He had a look of sheer delight on his face. He embraced me, kissed me, and I'll let you figure out the rest.

Let's back up a month or so and I'll fill in some of the details of how I found myself with Lee J. in the honeymoon suite of the Jack Tar Hotel in Galveston. We had set the date of our wedding for August 29, 1964. Of course, Mother was to make the bridesmaids' dresses, and I would wear Barb's wedding dress after it was altered.

I think I should interject a story here about my "going away suit." As you know, I was working for Interstate Securities. We had a regular solicitor who came by the office from time to time, always selling some very expensive women's clothing for more than reasonable prices. I had never bought anything from him, but one day, not too long before the wedding, he came by and showed me what I thought was the most beautiful three-piece double-knit suit I had ever seen. It was my size and fit perfectly. He offered it to me for thirty-five dollars. That was a lot of money for me, but it was a perfect going-away outfit. Except for some gifts from Lee J., nearly every piece of clothing I owned had been made by my mother. This three-piece suit was a real treat for me. I had no idea where the clothes this guy was selling came from or why he had them. I was not very wise to the ways of the world.

I later made some comments to my friend and a co-worker, Wanda, and she said, "You know those clothes he's selling are hot (stolen), don't you?"

In shock, I replied, "No!"

Wanda just laughed at how naïve I was. It was then that she kind of took me under her wing, and we became close friends. So, I was leaving on my honeymoon in stolen apparel. Oh, well!

I chose my three sisters and my friend, Alice Sitton, to be my bridesmaids. Lee J. had his brother, Tootie, his brother-in-law, Dan, and his friends, Ute Becton and Robert Reed, as his groomsmen. It was not to be a big elaborate wedding, but it was just right for us. Bro. Kendrick, our pastor from the local Baptist Church, was to officiate. For him to officiate a wedding, he included a mandatory counseling session. We met with him a week or so before the wedding. All I remember was that he was extremely sweet and kind. He had known both of us and our families for several years, so he knew our background well.

As our wedding day approached, we had to find an apartment. Lee J. suggested Tech Village. It was an apartment complex close to the campus strictly for married students. It was furnished but very bare bones. We thought it would be great. The price was $62 per month. Actually, it was cheaper than his dorm. We signed a lease, and it would be ours about a week before the wedding. I truly was getting excited.

Lee J.'s senior trip had been to Galveston at the Jack Tar Hotel. He showed me pictures of it and suggested we go there for our honeymoon. I thought it was a great idea, so we got reservations. We were all set. The Jack Tar turned out to be a great honeymoon retreat.

Getting our marriage license had a funny twist to it. Since we were both underage, we each had to have one of our parents sign for us. What a weird trip it was to the County Clerk's office. Lee J. and I sat in the front seat while both our "mommies" rode with us in the back seat, but we got our license. We could officially get "hitched." We did go to lunch together afterward, and it was all good. Mother was very pleased with me and my choice.

The wedding ceremony went off without a hitch. I have looked back at some of our wedding photos and the thing that struck me was how deliriously happy I appeared. That's because **I was**. The wait was over! The other thing about our wedding photos was how young we both looked. Of course, I was seventeen and Lee J. was twenty. We were young! As we exited the auditorium, he stopped and kissed me. It had finally happened; Lee J. and I were married in the eyes of the world, and we had the paperwork to prove it.

We had a wonderful reception after the ceremony in the fellowship hall of the church. It had been traditional in every way, the wedding cake, the throwing of the bouquet, and the throwing of the garter. After a memorable time with our family and friends, it was time to leave. We knew that some of our "friends" were going to try to sabotage our getaway, so Lee J. coerced his brother into helping us with our escape plans from the church. We would pretend we were going to leave in one vehicle, but instead, we would leave in Tootie's car with him driving. Earlier in the day, he had stashed our car at Wanda's house in Lubbock so we could leave from there. That was the plan.

After all the fanfare, Tootie brought his car around for our getaway. It was a traditional rice-throwing exit, and it was genuinely exciting as we made our way to the car. We both hopped in the backseat, and Tootie drove us away. We were soon at Wanda's house. We had pulled it off to perfection. Our "friends" were certainly disappointed because they'd had hopes of kidnapping Lee J. In Lubbock, we bid his brother goodbye, giving him a very heartfelt "thank you," and away we went.

On a side note, as we were preparing to leave the reception, Bro. Kendrick handed Lee J. an envelope and said it was something we might need. When we looked at it later, it was a certificate of marriage. I'm sure he thought we looked very young, and the certificate might come in handy; it did.

We had done it. After all the waiting we were a married couple. We drove out of Lubbock and headed south toward Snyder. That was where we were to spend our wedding night. I snuggled up as close to Lee J. as I could. I was happy beyond description, but another feeling was welling up inside me. I was feeling **free**. I've used this phrase before, but I felt like the bird that had been let out of its cage. I'll explain the freedom aspect of my feelings in more detail later.

I'm sure anyone would have thought there was only one occupant in the car as we headed south out of Lubbock. We arrived in Snyder in a little over an hour, and he got us a room at the Pal-O-Mar Cortel. It was the weirdest feeling for me when he unlocked the door, and we walked into our motel room. It was okay to be there; it was our wedding night. He brought in our luggage, and we sat on the bed for a few moments. Then, for the second time that night, he kissed me; I mean, he really kissed me.

I excused myself and went into the bathroom. I had bought a beautiful negligée and peignoir set. I undressed and put the negligée on but decided not to put the peignoir over it. The negligée was almost sheer; I wanted him to "see" me, all of me. When I came out of the bathroom, I saw that he had undressed and turned the covers back. As I entered the room, he couldn't take his eyes off me. He told me I looked more than just beautiful; he said I was just plain gorgeous. I really felt special when he said that.

We fell onto the bed and embraced. As we lay there, we kissed each other tenderly several times, and we both realized that we were exhausted. It had been a long day. I know this is weird, but we decided to wait until the next morning to consummate our union. We spent our wedding night with me lying in his arms. My naked body was nestled next to his as we lay together in the first real bed we had ever known as a couple. It was an incredible feeling to be in his arms for the whole night. I remember I didn't sleep very soundly, and each time I awoke, he was still there, our bare bodies still cuddled together. I was starting to feel something I'd not known before. No more goodnight-night kisses—those days were finally over.

When we began to awake the next morning, our need for each other was immediate. As we emerged from our sleep, we soon became one, and our union was consummated with lovemaking that was both tender and intense. My happiness knew no bounds.

The drive the next day took us to the Jack Tar Hotel and Resort in Galveston. As I said earlier, Lee J. had been there on his senior trip, and he thought it would make a great honeymoon retreat for us. As soon as I saw it, I loved it too. It was directly across the road from the beach. The pool and deck area was centrally located in the resort itself. I thought it was a very romantic place to be. The truth of the matter was that any place where we could be together 24/7 would have been a romantic place for me.

I'd had time to think during our drive to Galveston that day, and I realized that for the first time in my life, I was free of Mother's rules. Barb, Brenda, and myself (and later Kathy) all had the same restrictions to abide by, but my personality had **self-inflicted** additional pressure on myself to make sure that I strictly abided by her edicts. My naturally shy nature wanted no additional attention drawn toward me from her. I later realized that neither Barb nor Brenda felt the same pressure that I did. Barb would argue with Mother; I never did. Brenda would get mad and fight with Mother; I never did. They both had an outlet for their emotions; I just suppressed mine.

But now, here I was with Lee J. on our honeymoon, and I felt free, really free from all the restraints I had lived under my entire life. I especially felt free of the restrictions I'd followed since he and I had started dating almost exactly three years earlier. Looking back, Mother had never been unreasonable, and I understood that I was very young when I had fallen in love with Lee J., but now I didn't have to worry about any of that anymore. This new freedom I felt was very empowering and liberating. I could act on my feelings and it was okay. No longer did I feel the need to suppress my emotions as I'd been doing for years. **I could be me.**

He had arranged for us to stay in the honeymoon suite; the room cost us a whopping $25 per night. I know that because I found the receipt in some old mementos I've recently gone through. Of course, the staff knew we were honeymooners and treated us as such. I had never stayed in a hotel suite before, and it seemed very luxurious by my standards. The suite was two separate rooms, a bedroom, and a sitting room that included the bathroom that had a large **soaker tub for two** in it. It was a wonderful choice for us. We both would learn to love being in that tub together.

We got there Sunday afternoon late, and the plan was to stay four nights and three days. We went to check out the beach, but shortly, it was late afternoon. I discovered a life truth about myself. I loved the beach, just not the ocean. I found I much preferred the clear waters of the heated pool at the hotel rather than the waters of the gulf at the beach. There was a lot of seaweed on the beach, and it just gave me the creeps when some of it touched me when I was in the shallow water. I told Lee J. that I was sure that large creatures were always lurking nearby, just waiting to devour some young maiden. He teased me and said that, technically, I was no longer a maiden, so I shouldn't have to worry about something like that. He teased me a lot during our entire honeymoon, but I would learn some special ways to tease him back. That afternoon, I found myself in an almost giddy state; I was so happy.

Our first night at the Jack Tar was wonderful. When we went back to our suite after supper, I undressed and put my new negligée on once more, but this time, I put the peignoir on, too. It covered me somewhat so that I wasn't nearly as exposed. Lee J. seemed mesmerized by what he saw when I came through the door from the sitting room into the bedroom. He just sat on the bed and watched me. We both knew what we wanted, but I was enjoying a previously unknown freedom in my actions. Right now, I was very scantily clad in our honeymoon suite with my new husband. He had teased me earlier while we were on the beach, and now, I wanted to tease him a bit before I surrendered to our lovemaking. What a feeling!

As he sat there on the bed, I told him he could not touch me until I gave him permission. He just smiled and nodded okay. I started to kind of sway and pose a few feet away from him. I would open the peignoir a little and let him get a glimpse of what was underneath. I did this several times, and each time, I would let him see more than the time before, and then I would cover up again. (Okay, I was giving him a striptease, but I really had no idea how to do such a thing properly, however, what I was doing seemed to be working.) Yes, I could see the poor guy was getting quite "stimulated." I finally dropped the peignoir, and yet I still covered strategic parts of myself with my hands and arms. I gave him glimpses by moving them out of the way briefly. Shortly, off came the negligée. I let it drop to the floor, paused, and gave him what I thought was quite a seductive pose. I then walked over to him. I'll let you fill in the rest.

I learned a whole lot from that little episode. He told me later that what I'd done was the sexiest thing he had ever seen. He told me to feel free to "tease" him any time the mood struck me. I certainly filed that little bit of information away for later use. I don't know when I'd ever had more fun. I suppose it was the "freedom" thing I was feeling. I would soon learn that his playful teasing would generally be the verbal kind, while my forte would be more of the visual variety. Little did I know that I would soon have another opportunity. In fact, that opportunity would occur the very next morning. I described our activities in that episode to open this chapter. Such fun!

Once more, I have to say that I was the happiest I'd ever been in my entire life. Our honeymoon was turning out better than I ever could have imagined. We had an enjoyable morning together at the beach and later in the hotel pool. Since I had gotten a job to start the summer after my high school graduation, I'd not had a lot of time to get much of a tan, but I soon remedied that on the beach on our first day in Galveston. I mentioned that I had bought a two-piece bathing suit for our honeymoon, and I loved wearing it. I soon learned I could undo the backstrap on my top and tan my entire back for the first time ever. I had Lee J. rub some Coppertone on my back. His touch was quite sensuous, and it was all we could do to not head back to our suite for some more "activity." He found he could tease me by touching areas not associated with my back. (He was so "bad." He got really good at being "bad.") However, we held it together and remained on the beach until later.

After lunch, we headed to the pool. Lee J. stayed in the shade, but I continued to work on my tan. I had him apply some more Coppertone on me. Again, his application technique was more than a little naughty. Oh my, how I did love my new husband's touch as he applied the suntan oil! I had always been lucky that I didn't burn easily, and I had no issues with sunburn our entire honeymoon. I had a pretty good tan by the time we started home on Thursday.

One of our most memorable times occurred on Monday night. That night, out of nowhere, the hotel sent us a chilled bottle of champagne. Of course, neither of us had ever tasted champagne. I had never tasted an alcoholic drink of any kind before. Lee J. finally figured out how to pop the cork and poured each of us a little into the glasses that were provided. I took a sip and grimaced; I told him it was awful. He took a sip from my glass and agreed it was less than great, but since it was provided with the room, and this was our honeymoon, he thought he would just drink some of it. So, I watched and told him that he was an idiot to drink something that I thought tasted so awful. He drank a fair amount of it, and probably way too quickly. He thought drinking it was no big deal. **He was wrong.**

Shortly, instead of using the soaker tub and then embracing me as we had planned, he found himself embracing the toilet and puking his guts out. The champagne did not agree with him at all. The soaker tub and the lovemaking we had planned for later did not happen. Instead, it took him until the next morning to feel like himself again. I was more than a little peeved with him for being so **stupid** and ruining what we had planned for the previous night. It would not be the last time in our years together that I would get peeved with him when he did something that I considered stupid. Oh well, live and learn!

After the episode the night before, our honeymoon got back on track, and it continued to be everything a honeymoon was supposed to be. The next night, we did get to try out the large soaker tub in our suite. It obviously was made for two, and the hotel provided liberal amounts of bubble bath for our use. Lee J. said he had never had a bubble bath before in his life. I'd had a lot of them growing up, but I had never taken one with a good-looking naked guy in the tub with me. Needless to say, we did enjoy that tub, and again, I'll let you fill in the blanks for yourself.

Too soon, our time at the Jack Tar came to an end, so we headed home on Thursday. We drove three or four hours and decided to get a motel room for the night. We would finish the trip home on Friday. I don't remember where we were when we decided to stop for the night, but wherever it was, there were several motels to choose from. I picked the one where I wanted to stay, so he pulled into the port-a-call by the door. He went in and asked the guy at the front desk for a room with a king-sized bed. He looked at Lee J. and then looked at me, who he could see sitting in the car. Lee J. saw that he was a bit hesitant, so he asked him if a marriage certificate would help us get a room. He said, "It sure might."

Lee J. came out to the car and asked me to look in the glove box and hand him the envelope that Bro. Kendrick had given us. He took it inside to the guy at the desk and showed it to him. The guy just grinned and quipped, "You guys look awfully young!"

Lee J. said, "I know, but we got married last Saturday."

He filled out the paperwork for the room, and the desk guy gave him the key. As Lee J. was walking out, the guy quipped, "Have fun!"

Lee J. turned with a nod, grinning, and said, "I'm sure we will."

We did! The next morning we headed out once more and got to Lubbock midafternoon. Life as newlyweds was about to begin.

It makes me sad that we didn't take a camera with us on our honeymoon. We would have our first child (Julie) before snapshots and lots of pictures began happening. As I have said earlier, you'll just have to use your imagination and fill in the blanks.

So, how do I sum up the previous week's events? I had married the guy of my dreams, and we'd had a wonderful honeymoon together. We now found that our passion for each other had moved to a whole new level. I realized that I had not only married a wonderful guy, but I also was sure that he was a really good person. I was passionate about him as a person. Of course, there was the sexual side, but it had grown far beyond that. I realized that I was married to a guy who treated me wonderfully and loved me with every fiber of his being. We both were sure that we would be exclusive lovers for each other forever. How could I not have great passion for a person like that? All those qualities and more I would see and experience repeatedly in our coming years together. I sensed he had a similar passion for me. Of course, he was not perfect, nor was I. He will tell you that he could have a little selfish streak at times, but when it came to big decisions that involved me and later our kids, I was always sure he would make the best decision for "us," and he has.

Our honeymoon had allowed me to begin to shake off some of what I'd held deep inside myself for so long. Lee J. once asked me what was my main takeaway from our honeymoon, and I said, "Freedom" (hence the title of this chapter). It was the first time I'd felt free to allow myself to just "let go." And I found I enjoyed "letting go" and acting in ways I'd never allowed myself to do before. I certainly didn't understand it all myself; I just knew I loved it. I would realize as time passed that what had happened to me during those days would be the start of a long process to release the feelings and emotions I'd held inside myself since my childhood. Lee J. embraced this new side of me, which gave me even more freedom to explore myself when I found myself in circumstances that allowed expression. He told me he liked the new, more "complete" person that he saw in me. That gave me the confidence to allow that inner persona to emerge again when the time was right.

The giddy feeling of being 500 miles from home and feeling free to experience love and passion I'd not known before had been more than wonderful. We had created a great memory, but real life was about to start, but at least now, real life included us together. It was all good!

NOT WHAT I EXPECTED

Each workday morning, I dreaded going to work. I have mentioned that after my graduation in May from high school, I found a job as a cashier at a finance company, Interstate Securities. It was a small office with seven or eight employees; three were female, including me, and the rest were men in their late twenties or thirties. At the time I was seventeen and still living at home. I liked the other two female employees, especially Wanda. She was probably in her early thirties, and the other lady was in her twenties. I quickly learned my job, but now I found I was dreading going to work every day. I was young, pretty, innocent, and highly anxious. All these factors had a part in what I was starting to endure at work.

I was quite shy around the men in the office, and I certainly wasn't seeking their attention in any way. Wanda told me that my age and my looks were the reasons I was attracting their unwanted attention. I soon started to endure their off-color jokes and sexual innuendos that were directed toward me. Initially, it didn't happen every day; it was sporadic. But as my wedding day approached, it worsened. I had absolutely no clue how to handle their crude remarks.

The world I envisioned before our wedding date and the world I found myself in when we got back from our honeymoon weren't quite the same. In today's world, the environment at Interstate would be called "toxic," and what I was going through would be called "sexual harassment." I found myself in a very uncomfortable work environment. There was no HR department in those days, and women just had to endure that kind of environment if they were to keep their jobs, especially at Interstate.

The manager who had hired me and a couple of the other men who worked in the office had discovered how easily I became embarrassed and blushed. Coming back to work after the wedding and honeymoon, the off-color jokes and other sexual innuendos increased significantly. They made crude comments about our wedding night and what went on during our honeymoon. They made something that had been wonderful for me into something crass and distasteful. It made me feel awful. I felt like all I could do was blush and say nothing.

I was seventeen and had no idea how to handle the situation. Consequently, I soon grew to hate that job. I actually liked the work I did but hated the environment. The obvious question is, "Why didn't I just quit?" Two reasons: we needed the money and I was embarrassed. My shyness prevented me from telling anyone what was happening or asking what to do. As unhappy as I was, I just continued to tolerate it. Some days I would come home to the apartment and my stomach would be in knots. However, once I was home, it would get better. I was in a situation where I felt like I had to push through. I had to resort to the emotional suppression that I'd learned to do when I was growing up. The harassment didn't happen every day, but it happened often enough to make me a nervous wreck. As time went on, my embarrassment turned to anger. I once came home and told Lee J., "If I could, I'd kill those guys." I had become so angry it was affecting my health, but it was increasing my emotional toughness.

In addition to my situation, I soon learned when I got home from work each day that I had married a guy who had issues of his own that he was dealing with. He was trying to finish school in 3½ years and was taking a course load of 21 hours each semester. His problem was he didn't know what he wanted to do when he finished his degree, and he hated the courses he was taking. Let's just say that sometimes neither of us came home in a particularly good mood from my work environment and his school situation. The dream world I'd envisioned of marital bliss was not my world at all.

We loved each other to death, but we started arguing. I don't remember a single argument before we got married. We had mostly good times together, though, and I certainly preferred our married status over not being married. We were both experiencing and enjoying our overwhelming passion as newlywed lovers. We soon learned that "makeup sex" after an argument seemed to have an allure all its own. Just the very fact that I didn't have to say goodnight, and then he would leave, made all the difference for me. However, the situation was nothing like I had dreamed of or expected.

Upon reflection, there were some similarities between the work environment at Interstate and what I had dealt with as a kid growing up. I did have to deal with stress and anxiety in my world as a kid. In that world, I withdrew from the situation as quickly as I could. I went to my room and lost myself in a book. Now, as a young married woman, I found myself in a work environment that ramped up my stress and anxiety considerably. Eventually, it started to make me physically ill. It was very similar to what I had experienced as a kid. The big difference was that I had an apartment and a loving husband to go home to. Rather than immersing myself in a literary work of some kind, I lost myself in the arms of my husband and our extremely passionate sex life.

I think he was coping with his situation in the same way I was. We've looked back together and analyzed our situations through the prism of many years of life experiences together. We both agree that the coping mechanism for both of us was sex and lots of it. In each other's arms, we could, for a while, **make the world go away**. Lee J. says it reminds him of the old Jim Reeves song by that title.

Make the world go away, get it off my shoulders
Say the things you used to say, and make the world go away.
(*Make the World Go Away*, Jim Reeves)

Those lyrics say it all, and that's what we did!

I ended up working at Interstate for a little over a year. I had gotten pregnant in March of 1965, and we moved out of our apartment in Tech Village. In June, we rented a two-bedroom house. I finally got to quit my job at Interstate in late August after Lee J. started working a part-time job teaching guitar lessons. He was making more than enough for us to live on, so I had the opportunity to get away (escape?) from the environment at Interstate I so hated. The relief I felt was instant. Lee J. was due to graduate from Texas Tech, in December, the same month that our first child, Julie, was to be born. Things were looking up!

So, what was the takeaway from my experience working at Interstate? I found I'd had no choice but to resort once more to suppressing the very intense emotions I was dealing with. It was much the same as what I'd done during my years in elementary school. However, this time, my coping mechanism was immersing myself in the intense sexual activity with my ever-willing husband.

Some probably would say that a lot of sexual activity is normal for a newlywed couple. Without going into great detail, I can assure you that the frequency and intensity of our activity were probably not the norm for most couples. I'm sure the daily suppression of my emotions from work found some release in sex. Looking back, what I was going through resembled the best of times and the worst of times I recounted earlier. Only this time, the worst of times were during the day and the best of times were our nights.

If there was an upside to all the mental trauma, it would be that the experience toughened me up. I was forced to endure my situation when I felt that enduring it was my only option. I lost my innocence to the darker side of a world I'd never known before. I saw a side of life where some people can be downright cruel for no good reason. I now had experienced treatment from some really bad people from a world unprecedented to me. **Innocence lost is never regained.** So sad!

Rock-a-Bye-Baby

In the early morning hours of December 17, 1965, I started feeling "weird." I certainly didn't want to make a false alarm trip to the hospital, so I didn't wake Lee J. up until around 5 to 5:30 am. I told him we really needed to **go now!** As soon as we got to the hospital, the nurse took one look at me and said, "Girl, you're in labor!"

Julie Rae entered this world around 7 am. When they let Lee J. in to see me (this was before the days when the fathers were allowed in the delivery room), he said he had a final later that morning; I told him to go get that over with. I said I was tired but fine. He came back to the hospital after completing his final, and we went down to the nursery together. As we looked at Julie, he told me, "She's beautiful, just like her mother!" I agreed; she was beautiful. This had been a happy day. They kept me in the hospital for two days and then sent us home on the third. We went to my parent's house and stayed for about a week. I certainly needed that week to get ready to care for a newborn by myself.

Earlier, I spoke about my experiences as a newlywed when we lived in Tech Village. It was not the fairy tale I had imagined, but it was far better than Lee J. and me living separately. We hadn't specifically made a decision for me to try to get pregnant. I had begun taking birth control pills when we got married, and they were awful. They were nothing like the ones I took later. They made me gain weight, which I hated, and I just didn't feel good a lot of the time. After a few months, I quit taking them.

Wouldn't you know it, I got pregnant the next March after our wedding in August, and that was fine with me. As I've said, though this wasn't particularly planned, Lee J. seemed just fine with it, too. It soon became apparent that a one-bedroom apartment in Tech Village was not ideal for us with a new baby, so we started looking for a house to rent. We found one over on 26th Street close to the campus and rented it. It was not furnished, so we had to get some furniture. Then the fun began!

Back in those days, there were two furniture auction places that held auctions a couple of nights a week. In a little over a week's time, we bought a living room suite, coffee table and end tables, bedroom suite, mattress and box springs, dinette, TV, washing machine, and a refrigerator, and all that cost us around $300 **total**. Some of it was even new. The only thing that was a dud was the washing machine. Lee J. took it back and ran it through the auction again. He got almost all of what we had paid. I think we paid around $25 for it and got almost $20 back. We both had a blast furnishing that house.

We had an older couple as neighbors—the Petersons. Mrs. Peterson looked after me like a kind grandmother. She was always checking on me to see if I was doing OK. I continued working at Interstate and still hated the environment there. My friendship with Wanda made it easier to endure my boss and the other men who worked there. By the time we left Tech Village, I had toughened up a lot, and I could see a light at the end of the tunnel. I could soon quit the

Interstate job.

I was about to enter a time that seemed like I was caught up in a whirlwind. I was pregnant, we had a real house for me to fix up, Lee J. had found a great part-time job that he liked, and I had a date in mind when I could quit working at Interstate. It was a lot to process, and my anxiety could get ramped up at times. However, it was nothing like it used to be before we were married. The big difference was that we **were** married, and Lee J. was a big help when he could see me getting wound up. I could tell he really loved me, and I really loved him!

I'll share a little about the job Lee J. had found. He and his brother had started taking guitar lessons when they were in elementary school, and he had become a pretty good "picker." He crossed paths with his old guitar teacher, Earl Swinford, about the time we left Tech Village. Earl offered him a part-time job, and he took it. That turned out to be great. He was making really good money for a part-timer, and he enjoyed it. It took him away from me some afternoons and evenings, but financially, it eased things a lot. Since I was pregnant, the extra money was needed, and I started to really anticipate becoming a mom. Even though I hated my job environment, I could be happy when I was away from there and with Lee J.

When the fall semester started, I quit my job at Interstate, and that was a big relief. Earl had made Lee J. a good deal to work for him, teaching and preparing music, paying a good commission on any sales he made. This was Lee J.'s last semester at Tech before his graduation. Once more he was taking more than a full load and working part time.

After I quit working at Interstate, my life was so much better, and I had a baby to get ready for. I started preparing a nursery, and I specifically remember the tiered window curtains I made for it. I thought they were so cute. I got the bassinet Mother had bought for Barb when she had Kristi. It turned out that it would be passed around our family for years. Our little nursery wasn't fancy, but then again, I wasn't used to fancy. This was such fun.

With Lee J.'s graduation looming in December, the big question became, "What now?" Lee J. had decided that he did not want to pursue a job in the field of agronomy. He was a farm boy who no longer had a passion for agriculture. I don't know why this happened, but it did. Working part time, he was making close to the starting salary of someone with his degree if they went to work for a seed or chemical company. However, he was enjoying teaching guitar to kids. So, he got the idea to see if he could do something like what his boss was doing. He'll tell you now, it was a hairbrained idea, but that was what he was going to try.

He talked with Earl about a location where a guitar school like Earl's might do well. Earl was familiar with the lack of guitar studios in Amarillo and suggested that the area might be a good choice for one modeled after the one he had in Lubbock. Years earlier, he had built a studio complex at his home in west Lubbock. Lee J. got the idea to check out Amarillo. Without going into detail, over the next few months, his idea of a guitar studio in Amarillo started to take shape.

I guess my shape was changing, too, since I was due in

December. I was happy and excited but more than a little bit anxious about becoming a mom. Lee J. was trying to wind up his final semester, and I was due about the same time as his finals were scheduled. So, we had that to possibly contend with. Sure enough, as I related earlier, that's what happened.

When we went back to our house in Lubbock after our stay in Idalou, our lives had been changed forever! We now had our own child, and Lee J. was a college graduate. We soon realized that babies do not come with an owner's manual. We were really two kids with a kid of our own. My new world was unlike anything I'd ever known before, but I was happy.

It would be February before things were ready for us to move to Amarillo. I thought the idea of a guitar studio in the converted garage of the house his dad had bought sounded just fine. He just needed to acquire the number of students that would make the studio business successful. I loved the idea because he would be home most of the time. So, it was Amarillo, here we come!

It had been about a year and a half since we had gotten married, and my world had been nothing like what I'd dreamed it would be. It wasn't bad, it was just far different than I had imagined. We were moving to Amarillo; we had a new baby; Lee J. was stepping out into something new that neither of us had even thought about a year earlier. I was happy and learning to be a mom. Though things were uncertain, life was good. Amarillo was to be a transition time that had its ups and downs, too.

AMARILLO
(From Musician to Pilot)

It was a Sunday afternoon in August 1966 when a seemingly small event occurred that would begin to change everything. Lee J. saw an advertisement in the Amarillo paper from the local Cessna Pilot Center for a $5 introductory flight lesson. On a lark, we drove out to the Tradewinds Airport. He took the $5 flight lesson, and our world changed forever. A seed was planted that day that would take us in the direction neither of us had ever dreamed of nor thought about. Nothing changed abruptly, but the seed had been sown. For the next few months, Lee J. took a few lessons along, and after Christmas, he decided to look for a part-time job to make enough extra money to finish up his private license. He took a job as a Fuller Brush man selling their items door to door. He passed his check ride in April.

Since moving to Amarillo, our lives required some adjustments. It seemed parenthood would do that. I found I loved being a mom. Lee J. had been busy since the move, getting the guitar studio up and running, and he was succeeding. By the time he took that flight lesson, I was truly loving being a mom. I was happy, and he seemed to be too. My anxiety wasn't much of a problem, and the biggest thing was I felt unshackled from all the rules I once lived under. Amarillo was only about one hundred miles from Idalou, but that was far enough I felt free to be "me." I think Lee J. and I both liked being "us," but now "us" included three, not two people. Julie was now such a part of our lives that I couldn't imagine life without her; she was changing so fast. While Lee J. spent his late afternoons teaching, I spent my time taking care of Julie, which included playing with her. I was truly content.

Lee J. came from a generation where the moms did basically all of the childcare. He did learn to help feed Julie and was always fascinated by just watching her. I would sometimes bring her in and lay her in the bed with us. What a realization for me to think that we had made this little baby. We both thought that she was so beautiful. He would tell me, "She's beautiful just like her mother." It thrilled me to hear him say that.

Our personal life took a little adjustment, though. We were no longer passionate newlyweds in a single-bedroom apartment in Tech Village. We had graduated to being parents, so we took on the responsibilities that came with parenthood. I was becoming a mom who loved her new role; Lee J. was a clueless new dad. He has told me as he looks back now, he wishes he had been more hands-on like our grandsons are with their kids today. But he was from a far different time and generation. He did get better at helping me as Julie got a little older.

Due to the nature of the guitar studio business, it seemed that now we had more time together than we'd had in quite a while. As had been the case in times past, if we had time together, our passion for each other would inevitably rise.

Things were no different now. I hoped I was still the lover I had become while we lived in Tech Village. But since I was now both a wife and mother, there were a few modifications. Before Julie came along, our time for lovemaking (if we were at home) was basically "if we felt like it, that's what we did." Now, it was somewhat different, if only because of Julie's feeding schedule. She generally slept soundly right after she ate, so if we were in the mood, we would take our opportunities shortly after she had her bottle. The fact Lee J. was at home during the day gave us a fair amount of flexibility. Let's just say we took advantage of it pretty regularly.

The other change in the area of our sex life had to do with how totally involved I could be in our lovemaking. In times past, I was 100% into it. Now, it was more like 90%. No matter the passion of the moment, there was a part of me tuned to the sound of the first whimper or cry from Julie's baby bed. If I heard or sensed anything, I would tell Lee J. something like, "Hold that thought, I need to check on Julie." I know it had to be frustrating for him from time to time, but I would return as quickly as I could. Honestly, the interruption was equally frustrating for me, too. However, our passion for each other remained high.

That first summer in Amarillo was the first time since leaving home that I could "lay out" a lot and enjoy getting a tan. I had fully recovered my figure since Julie's birth and had started exercising regularly. Lee J. had learned his lesson that compliments were a part of my love language. He complimented me regularly, though often he would revert into his teasing mode, which, if heard by others, would probably seem quite inappropriate. He could be really "bad." Either way, I loved his words, and I loved him.

It was about the time that Lee J. got his private license that the house next door came up for sale. Lee J. and Tootie approached their dad about buying it. The plan was for Tootie and Ann to move to Amarillo and join Lee J. in the guitar studio business. I really don't remember how I felt about the business situation, but I really enjoyed having Ann's company. We did a lot of things together, and it was good having them next door. They went to work, increasing their student load. Initially, though, Lee J. gave Tootie some of his students, which forced a drop in income for us. I don't remember exactly how much, but some. It was when this occurred that I started having some anxiety issues again. It wasn't overwhelming, but it did become an underlying worry I had to deal with.

I now know that the guitar business was never something Lee J. thought he would do for a lifetime. He was a kid with a college degree in a field he had no desire to participate in. He has told me and others that in the last year and a half of college, he felt like a ship with no rudder, just drifting. Well, when he graduated from Tech, our ship drifted to Amarillo and the guitar business. That flight lesson he had taken earlier was a seed that had been planted, and now it had sprouted and started to grow.

During the last months of getting his private pilot's license, Lee J. started thinking about getting his commercial and instructor licenses and then transitioning into a career in aviation. The one thing that became apparent to me was, for the first time since I had known him, he had a real passion for something he was doing. I was even excited because the guy I loved finally saw something that excited him (besides me). Little did I know that there would be a hefty price for us to pay for him to get those two licenses.

Not too long after our move to Amarillo, we traded our old Pontiac in for a 1966 GTO. I really loved that car. My life was beginning to smooth out pretty well, and as I said previously, I was content. However, Lee J. dropped a bombshell on my newly found contentment. To get both of his needed licenses, he was required to log approximately 175 additional flight hours. The cost would be at least $2,500. That was a lot of money for us back then. The only thing we had that would get us that kind of cash was our GTO.

Kenneth Brown, the owner of Amarillo Flying Service, proposed to swap his old 1958 DeSoto sedan for our one-year-old 1966 GTO in return for enough credit to enable Lee J. to get his commercial and instructor's rating. I reluctantly agreed to it, but I hated driving that old car; I mean, **I really hated that old car**. He kept teaching guitar and started logging flight hours. It took him from May until early October, but he obtained his commercial pilot license and became a certified flight instructor. He could now be paid for his flying.

About this time, I had begun thinking about having another baby. I'm not sure Lee J. was gung-ho about having another mouth to feed at this time, **but** things happen. Again, like before with my pregnancy with Julie, I quit taking my birth control pills. The frequency of our "encounters" pretty well guaranteed I would soon be pregnant. In our case, I got pregnant in the fall of 1967.

As soon as he was rated, Mr. Brown started giving Lee J. as many students and charter flights as he could, but we soon learned it wasn't enough. Even though Lee J. was still teaching guitar, he couldn't fly and teach very easily. Mr. Brown tried to give us some help by hiring me to be the office bookkeeper and answer the phone at the airport office. However, his wife was an office micro-manager who made my life miserable. I was already miserable enough because I was pregnant again, and I hated leaving Julie in daycare even though she was with Ann. Add to that, money was extremely tight. As miserable as I was, I knew this situation wouldn't last forever. I had become a lot tougher than I had once been. I think my experience at Interstate had helped me a lot in that area. Things would soon change in ways I'd never imagined.

Lee J. was becoming more and more assured that aviation would be his field of choice. I sensed his happiness in what he was doing, and I loved that for him. However, my anxiety about our precarious financial situation was taking a toll on me, but that would soon change.

In early April 1968, Lee J. happened to be in Lubbock on a flight. While on the ground with some time to kill, he walked into the office of the T-41 program at the Lubbock Airport. He knew very little about what the T-41 job entailed, but he did learn he was qualified for it. The salary was significantly more than he was making in Amarillo. He left an application with them for an instructor's job while he was there. Two days later, they called and said they just had a position come open. Did he want it? The answer was an immediate "Yes!" This meant we would be leaving the guitar business behind with Tootie. Lee J., myself, and Julie would be moving back to Idalou with a real job with set hours, a known schedule, and a guaranteed paycheck. My world was starting to fall into place. I could hardly believe it.

But first, I'd like to recap our twenty-six-month excursion to Amarillo. It was a mixed-bag experience. I began as the wife of a guitar teacher; I left as the wife of a flight instructor teaching Air Force student pilots from Reese AFB to fly the T-41 in Lubbock, Texas. We had some good times in Amarillo. Lee J. and I were together a lot. Especially more than those last months while he finished Tech. I liked that. When Ann and Tootie moved to Amarillo, I loved being with Ann, and any loneliness I'd experienced when we first arrived there was gone. I also loved learning to become a mom for Julie.

However, the financial hardships we endured during those last months were certainly not pleasant. In fact, upon looking back, they were **awful;** as was my time working at the office at the airport. Lee J. has admitted that the selfish streak in his personality was a big factor in putting all of us through a tough time financially for a while. However, he was always sure it was temporary. He was so sure that he was on the right track for what he was destined to do that he did what he did. He's told me repeatedly he sincerely regretted us having to go through that. Of course, enduring the uncertainties of what our future would look like kept my anxiety working overtime. But it was what it was, and I think our little family left Amarillo much better than when we moved there. I knew I was stronger for it, but it was a welcome relief to be moving back to Idalou.

YOU WANT US TO DO WHAT?

It was around Thanksgiving when Lee J. dropped a stunning proposal on me. After training Air Force student pilots for about eight months, he started thinking about his future in aviation. If possible, he knew he wanted flying to be his life-long career, but the T-41 job had no long-term future. He was building flying time, but it was not the kind of experience he would need to progress to any type of pilot job except to be an instructor somewhere else. He was certain he did not want to be an instructor forever. In talking with his students, he realized that he was as qualified as any of them to become a rated Air Force pilot. The good jobs in aviation were primarily taken by ex-military pilots after leaving the service, which left guys like him getting lower-paying instructor jobs. So he proposed that **we** join the Air Force and take that route to a career for him in aviation. **I was stunned!** Hence, the title of this chapter. Never in my wildest dreams had I ever thought about him/us in the military, but that was his proposal.

All I could think of was that the Vietnam War was going on, and I was afraid of losing my husband and the father of my kids. He explained his rationale. He thought that his experience as a T-41 instructor had not only taught him how to fly the Air Force way but it had also taught him how to be a great student. He was sure that with this knowledge, he could graduate from pilot training with a class ranking that would allow him to pick what he called a "non-combat" assignment. The higher a person's class rank, the more likely that person would get the assignment of his choice. His idea at the time was an assignment to fly cargo, aerial tankers, and such. This, of course, would lead to a sure airline job when he got out. He made it all sound so simple. He also was convinced that if the caliber of some of his students was any indicator of how well he would do, he would excel at it. (He'd had some students that he said were some real dummies, but they were going to get their wings soon.) Well, that was my husband, the man of supreme confidence. Once on the flight line, the pay in the Air Force and the benefits would soon outstrip his T-41 salary.

As it turned out, he was right about how well he would do. He did get his assignment of choice. The process of getting me on board did take some time, though. Throughout most of December and into January, we talked about it a lot. I began to realize that the man I loved, unlike me, was totally unafraid to take on a challenge like this. He was smart, capable, and ambitious. I was still dealing with my anxiety and shyness, but I was far better at handling those issues than in the past. Recently, I looked back at the biography I had written nine years earlier for my 50th high school class reunion. I reread my words and was struck by the fact that I said, "OK, let's go for it!" I also said, "I think I realized that I too had a bit of longing to have some adventure in my life."

How did we get to this point? Let me go back to the start when Lee J. got the T-41 job. What a rapid change! We were in Amarillo one week, and then he started a new job in Lubbock the next. Needless to say, I was elated, but what an overwhelming turn of events for a seven-and-a-half-month pregnant twenty-one-year-old "girl." We packed a few clothes and headed to my parents' house for that weekend. On the way, I started trying to figure out how to make all this happen as smoothly as possible. It all worked out. An apartment was available on 4th Street in Idalou, and we rented it that weekend. My mother said she would keep Julie while Raymond and Gwen, Lee J.'s parents, would take me back to Amarillo to get our stuff packed up. I went with them on Monday, and we started packing on Tuesday. We finished up and loaded on Wednesday. It all went in one U-Haul trailer, and we were back in Idalou late that day. Lee J started his initial training on that Monday and took his check ride the following Monday. We were all set. What a week!

And so began a new saga for me. I was so happy to be back close to home, and for the first time in a long while, Lee J. was making a good living and loving what he was doing. The obstetrician who delivered Julie agreed to be my doctor again, even though I was over seven months along. Mother came by every morning to check on me, and on May 14, as we sat in our living room talking, I felt something. I immediately told her we had better get to the hospital. I called Lee J.'s work number and told them to let him know my mother and I were headed for the hospital. He was on his first flight of the day and didn't know what was going on immediately. When he got the word, he headed for the hospital and barely got there before I delivered. It was less than two hours from my first twinge to a delivered baby girl we named Angie Lea. Lee J. teased me that I would have been a great Wild West frontier-type woman. I could have had a baby in the morning, and then I could have gone back to work in the fields that afternoon. Personally, I didn't think it was all that funny. I guess I've been blessed to have babies so easily.

As usual for those times, I stayed in the hospital for three days. We then went to my folks' house for a few days. I'll admit, the second time around was easier than the first, as I didn't feel so stupid about taking care of a newborn. Lee J. was loving his new job, and I was loving being back home where I had some help. A duplex right down the street came open soon after Angie was born, and we took it. I felt like we were becoming a cozy little family. I was happy.

Lee J. came home soon after Angie was born and said he was trying to right a wrong he had thrust upon me in Amarillo. Someone at work had a 1966 Chevrolet Impala for sale, and he had made an offer. He said we should go look at it together. It wasn't my GTO, but it was nice, so we bought it. He got rid of the hated old Desoto and bought a really cheap clunker for a work car. I remember the bumper rattled on it, and Julie could hear him when he turned down our street by the Dixie Dog. She would tear out the door and go running to meet him. She would grab onto his leg, and he would walk her into the house with her hugging his leg. She loved it! He loved it! Life was good.

I think this is as good a time as any to convey to all to read how I felt about this guy whom I had married almost four years earlier. I was more in love with him than ever before. Oh, I could get mad at him for a time, but it never lasted very long. He loved his job in the T-41 program, and he loved his kids and me. He let Julie wrap him around her little finger. He even wrote a song about her and called it *"Daddy's Little Girl."* Of course, Angie was way too small to have the kind of interactions with him that Julie did. But I swear, I've never seen a young man who loved little girls like he did. I think he got that from his dad. His dad would crack up when Julie sang Lee J.'s revamped version of the Zacchaeus song for him. Let's just say that the original version did not have the word "hiney" in it.

Our passion for each other had never seemed to wane. I made getting the kids in bed a top priority so we could go to bed. We loved our kids, but we loved our own bedtime, too! In Lee J.'s autobiography, he expounds a bit on his feelings about this time. The following is a direct quote from his autobiography.

"Though she was now a great mom for Julie and Angie, she was also an ever-willing lover for me. Every man should be so blessed! My entire world and especially my world with Sandy just felt right. Sometimes, the words in a song say what I am feeling far better than any words that I might write. The words to a song made popular by Alabama, "Feels So Right," tells it all for me.

Whisper to me softly, breathe words upon my skin
No one's near and listening, no need to say goodbye
Just hold me close and love me, press your lips to mine
Mmmm, feels so right, feels so right
Lying here beside you, I hear the echoes of your sighs
Promise me you'll stay with me, and keep me warm each night
Hold me close and love me, press your lips to mine
Mmmm, feels so right, feels so right
Your body feels so gentle and my passion rises high
You're loving me so easy, your wish is my command
Just hold me close and love me, tell me it won't end
Mmmm, feels so right, feels so right"

(*Feels So Right*, Alabama)

Every time I read those words, I fall in love with him again. Everything did feel so right.

I truly did love being back close to home, but it also meant I felt my mother's presence when I would do something new or maybe out of the ordinary. It was kind of unspoken, though, "Would Mother think this was okay?" I would learn much later that I was **subconsciously** and unnecessarily carrying Mother's rules from my childhood into my adulthood.

It was in August, after our move back to Idalou, that we got caught up in some of my family's drama. My younger sister Kathy had to tell Mother and Daddy that she was pregnant. No one knew she had even been dating the baby's father. One can imagine the turmoil this caused. Mother was beside herself! We were part of the discussion of what to do after the news was out. The father of the baby was an Idalou boy who was in college at Tarleton State University, located in Stephenville, Texas. He knew nothing about the pregnancy, so it was decided that someone needed to go to Stephenville to tell him. Somehow, Lee J. was selected to be the messenger. He was fine with it, and late that afternoon, we headed to Stephenville.

I'm almost ashamed to admit this, but I thought we could make this trip a short vacation for us. Here I am saying it again, "I felt like I was the bird that had just been let out of its cage." Lee J. and I had not had a night away from home without the kids since they were born. He didn't seem to be the least bit nervous about his role as the designated bearer of bad news. The plan was to spend the night in Stephenville after he delivered the news to the father-to-be. I guess I was feeling a little "naughty" when I suggested to my more-than-willing husband that we could be honeymooners again for one night. He thought about it for about half a second and said that it sounded like a great idea, but first, he had his messenger business to attend to.

It took us a while to locate the person we needed to see, but we did find him. Lee J. delivered the message to a somewhat stunned and bewildered young college student. Once our business was done, we found a nice motel. I told Lee J. to ask for a room with a king-sized bed. This would become my standard request for years to come. He would always tease me and ask, "Does this mean you're planning on **needing** a large playground?"

I would emphatically tell him, **"Yes-it-does!"**

I made sure we both enjoyed a very "uninhibited" one-night second honeymoon. I guess, as the saying goes, "If you're served a lemon, make some lemonade."

It would be a while after the turmoil over Kathy's pregnancy issue quieted down that Lee J. dropped the proposal described at the beginning of this chapter on me. Things were good with his job instructing in the T-41 program, but he could see that he needed a plan for the long term, and the Air Force seemed like a possibility.

Looking back now, I'm sure that I had something deep inside me that was beginning to stir. I really was happy to be where we were at the moment he suggested that "we" join the Air Force. Yet, after discussing his proposal for a few weeks, I began to feel like I might like a little travel and adventure for myself. Little did I know just how much adventure we would share in the next five years. Some of it very good and some not so good, however, the good far, far outweighed the bad. I should add here that he told me from the start that unless I was 100% on board with his desire to join the Air Force, he would drop it. I knew if we followed his proposal, it would ramp up my anxiety since it would all be so new and different for me, but the stirring I was feeling deep inside was also intriguing. So I agreed to it, and we did it. We would be an Air Force family.

Sometime in January 1969, Lee J. started the process of joining the Air Force. It involved a series of mental and intellectual tests along with a medical exam. He passed everything with flying colors, except he had impacted wisdom teeth. They would have to be removed. He got that done, and his application was accepted. My world was being turned upside down. There was nothing initially to do because his OTS date wasn't until mid-May. (That later got changed to the 9th of June.) That gave us four months to prepare for Lee J,'s leaving for OTS. I knew the ninety days of OTS would be hard, but they turned out to be far harder than I ever imagined.

For those who read this and don't know the process of training an Air Force pilot, here is a brief synopsis. To fly in the Air Force, a person must become a commissioned officer. The route to a commission for Lee J. was through the Air Force Officer Training School, OTS. It was a ninety-day school about all things military. It involved physical training, academics, learning to march, and working as a team. I think you get the idea. Lee J. will tell you there was nothing fun about it. In talking to his T-41 students, they explained it was all a big game to weed out those who weren't cut out to be Air Force officers. It was a three-month process to be endured, but once out of there and in the real Air Force, as they called it, the good stuff starts (flying airplanes).

Lee J. continued to work at his job in T-41s while we figured out what I should do when he would be in San Antonio. Since an OTS student's pay scale was about half what he was making as a civilian, I needed to find a job. I got a job at Travelers Insurance Company in March. We hired Elsie Caudle to keep the kids during the day. She was the sweetest woman, and she loved our girls. Working at Travelers was good. It kept me busy while Lee J. was gone, plus the extra money helped us have a little nest egg for his time in OTS. A plan emerged that I would live with Mother and Daddy and work at Travelers while he was in OTS. My mother agreed to keep the kids.

We thought we needed a vacation before Lee J. had to leave. We decided to go to Six Flags with Barb and Dan and their kids in May and we did have a good time. However, the thought of a three-month separation from him was always there in the back of my mind. I knew it would be hard; little did I know how hard! More about that later.

As the time drew near for him to leave, we wanted to spend as much time together as possible. The weekend before he left, we took the kids to Silver Falls for a day. I had seen a cute, sexy outfit in one of the downtown women's stores earlier while doing a little shopping during my lunch hour at Travelers. We were in town a couple of days later, and I showed it to him. Of course, he loved it and bought it for me. He knew I needed a bit of cheering up. It was something I wouldn't normally wear around my mother, so I wouldn't get a chance to wear it again until I saw him in San Antonio halfway through his training.

As his day of departure drew closer, I found myself missing him already, and he wasn't even gone. Since we had started dating almost eight years earlier, we had never been apart for more than a couple of days here and there. To say I was miserable inside would be a gross understatement, but I think I was able to hide it from him and my family members to some extent. We stayed in our duplex right up until the time he was to leave, so we still had our privacy. I found myself wanting to make love with him every possible moment we could. I guess I thought it was something I could store up, like a deposit in a savings account. I was wrong!

Writing about this time in our lives has left me feeling incredibly sad. Not that it wasn't a terribly sad time for me, because it was. But I think I may be viewing my memories of this time through the lens of a 78-year-old great-grandmother and not the lens of the 23-year-old "girl" that I was. I think my youth had a way of making me more resilient in some ways than I would be if I faced the same situation at my current age. I think my ability to suppress my emotions actually came in handy during this time. Once more, I was adding hidden emotional baggage to my subconscious psyche.

As hard as it was then, it would be way more difficult today. Lee J. and I depend on each other so much more now because of our age. As we've talked about this, he told me he couldn't mentally (or physically, of course) go through OTS again at his current age. Nor do I think I could go through a similar ninety-day separation from him at my age now. We both know that it is likely that one of us will face a permanent separation from the other sooner or later but I choose to think about that tomorrow at Tara (family joke).

With this realization, I hope I can keep the perspective I had in my youth rather than that of my current age as I continue to put down my memories of a time now long past. I've reread what I've written to date. I've edited it a bit here and there, and I'm satisfied that my words do express who I was at that time in my life.

Separation

Since I had spent the night at the hotel, my bag was already in our room, so I handed Lee J. the key and hurriedly showed him the way. He tried to talk to me as I rushed him down that sidewalk, but I was hardly listening. As we entered the room and closed the door, I said, "Would you please shut up!"

He dropped his bag, getting the hint that talk would have to come later. I immediately started to unbutton his shirt. Normally, about now, I would tell whoever reads these words that I'll let you fill in the rest, but because this situation was so unique for us, I'm providing more information than I normally would.

We fell onto the bed and quickly undressed each other; our passions began to dictate our actions. I must admit, I had never experienced making love with my husband like what we shared that morning in San Antonio. I had so much pent-up inside me, and these moments provided an outlet for their release. As we began making love, the emotions boiled to the surface. Our passion grew, and I completely lost myself. I became frantic and vocal in a way I'd never known. Shortly, waves of ecstasy and satisfaction swept over us both. I didn't want to stop, and I begged him not to. He didn't. We continued, and soon, I climaxed once again. I was thoroughly exhausted. I remember clinging to him as he held me in his arms; I began to sob quietly. I also found him sobbing with me and **for** me. Without a doubt, this had been one of the "take my breath away" moments that I've never forgotten. Finally, we talked.

I showed him some new pictures of the kids and me. Upon seeing them, he told me how he longed to gather all three of us in his arms for a huge group hug. As we talked, I told him how lonely I had been even though I was surrounded by my family. I told him that sometimes I cried myself to sleep and didn't know how I got up the next morning and went to work. But I did. I asked him a little about OTS, but he didn't have much to say. He told me it was a big game that he was playing and felt he was playing it pretty well; mainly, he was just **enduring** it. He told me, thank goodness, that he was halfway through it.

While talking, we were still lying naked on the bed. I moved toward him, and he knew I needed him once more. So, we made love again, only this time far more tenderly. (What an incredible guy I had married!) We'd learned before he left for OTS that sex wasn't something we could store up, but for those two days, we certainly tried—again, to no avail. We did create some wonderful memories to help us through the next weeks of his OTS training. Little did we know these memories would last a lifetime; memories which are now being converted into words for the first time ever.

Lee J. had left on June 9, 1969, for the induction center in Amarillo before going to Lackland AFB in San Antonio for his 90-day training to become an officer in the USAF. So began the longest separation that Lee J. and I had ever had since we started dating in the summer of 1961. Needless to say, they turned out to be the hardest three months of my life.

I found myself back living with my parents, but now I had two kids. My sister, Kathy, had had her baby, Karla, six months earlier and was with us too. I really didn't know what I was getting myself into when I asked Mother and Daddy if my kids and I could stay with them during Lee J.'s absence at OTS. I quickly learned that Kathy and Karla were Mother's first priority. Nothing was ever said, but the feeling of being in the way was pervasive. Mother did have her hands full with my two and a six-month-old to care for during the day. Neither Mother nor Daddy ever said anything until I was getting ready to go to see Lee J. in July. He could not leave the base until the first period of training time was over. It seemed like an eternity.

Looking back, I know Mother was overwhelmed. I tried to help in every way I could after returning from work. I don't remember if Kathy was working or not, but I do think Mother was still an emotional wreck from Kathy's unwed pregnancy. Now she had me and my crew to deal with. It was just a bad situation that had no good solution until Lee J.'s graduation in early September.

As for me, I was also an emotional wreck. I think being separated from Lee J. during this time was the worst thing I had ever had to deal with. Even though I was in a house full of people, I was terribly lonely. Many nights, I cried myself to sleep; I had no one to talk to; I had no one to share my thoughts with. I so wanted to close my eyes and lie in his arms again. I have to will myself out of bed every morning. The job, though, was good; it kept me busy and restricted my mind from dwelling on Lee J. much during the day. I never complained to Mother or Daddy, using my ability to suppress my emotions and put on a good face. However, as I've said, I was an emotional wreck.

I learned that Lee J's first weekend to get off base would be July 19-20. As I said earlier, neither of my parents had said anything until then. This time, Daddy was not happy when I told him I had to see Lee J. and that I would be gone for three days. For the first time ever, he got mad at me. He said that Mother was overwhelmed. I knew she was, and I felt bad, but I had to see my husband. Lee J. had gone through the induction center in Amarillo with a fellow OTS trainee named Bob Comolli. His wife, Nancy, was going to San Antonio to see Bob the same weekend I planned to go, and she offered me a ride with her. I took her offer.

We went down on Friday afternoon and got rooms at the Albert Pick Hotel. The guys got a ride from the base bus service and got to the hotel about 9 am Saturday morning. You can't imagine the elation I felt when I threw my arms around Lee J. The opening paragraphs of this chapter tell of our passion just minutes later as we got to our room.

For a brief weekend, all was right in my world! We would have until 5 pm Sunday when the guys had to sign back in at the base. Even after over 50 years, my memories of those two days remain vivid. We spent our time in one of three places: the hotel room, the beautiful pool, or the River Walk.

The Albert Pick Hotel was a beautiful place to be. I had bought a new bikini for the weekend in San Antonio; the pool there was gorgeous. With the situation at home, I had no time to get my usual summer tan. I spent some time sunning during those two days, desperately needing the relaxation that the pool offered.

From what I've already written, you are aware of the sexual passion that Lee J. and I shared from early on in our relationship. It doesn't take a mental giant to figure out that after several weeks of separation, we spent a lot of time during those two days behind closed doors. Unlike our first sexual encounter, others were far less frantic. It was an incredible two days!

I guess we were too cheap or broke to rent a car, so we used the hotel shuttle service to get down to the River Walk that Saturday night. I'd never heard about the San Antonio River Walk before that night, but some of the guys in his OTS squadron had told Lee J. about it. That Saturday night, we discovered it and the Casa del Rio Café for ourselves. I thought then and still do now that it was the most romantic place I could have ever imagined. It was fantastic since I got to experience it with my husband that weekend. It was a perfect place to wear the sexy outfit he had bought just before he left for San Antonio. He told me more than once how beautiful he thought I looked wearing it. He could make me feel so special.

I suppose our situation at that moment had something to do with the way I felt. I just couldn't soak it all in. Since that time, over 50 years ago, we've visited the River Walk quite often, but nothing compares to my memories of that night. It certainly was something special for both of us.

We caught the shuttle around 9 pm and went back to the hotel. One night just wasn't enough! As wonderful as our lovemaking was, I couldn't shake the nagging feeling of leaving him again the next afternoon. It was a mixed feeling of incredible delight and sadness all at once. I remember lying in his arms as he held me close all that night. We spent all the next day at the hotel. Neither of us wanted to go anywhere.

Too soon, Sunday afternoon came through, and we had to say goodbye once more. I was incredibly sad as Nancy and I got into her VW bug for the ride home. I don't remember us talking much. I certainly didn't feel like talking, and suddenly, I was incredibly tired. We got back to Idalou sometime before midnight. Of course, Daddy was worried as he always was, but he was glad to have one of his chickens safely back home in the roost. The next morning, my routine started once again. But now I have wonderful memories of us from the previous weekend. It seemed to help some.

I guess now is as good a time as any to talk about the letters that flew back and forth between Lee J. and me. We didn't write every day, but we both had quite a pile of letters when he graduated to go along with some "compromising" photos of me that we had made. Many years later, we read them again. He thought we should get rid of them because we were both quite explicit in our writings. He didn't think the kids should read them. I didn't want to destroy them, and we didn't for a while. I relented a while later, and we trashed the letters and a lot of the photos. (We did keep the ones from our second honeymoon in the Bahamas in 1973.) I do wish now that we had kept them. He does, too.

The uncomfortableness of living at my parent's house was unceasing. I continued to learn that Kathy would always have priority from my parents. As Daddy would say, "Some people need more help than others." Looking back at it now, that was really a backhanded compliment to me. My daddy certainly didn't think that I needed the kind of help they gave Kathy and her kids in the years to come. Nor would I have wanted it.

The plan was for me to go back to San Antonio in four weeks for the weekend of August 16-17. As that time drew close, Daddy was having a fit that I was going to drive there by myself. His anxiety just made everything that much worse, but I knew I had to see Lee J. again. Barb volunteered to keep Angie that weekend, which helped my spirits a bit. It probably helped Mother, too. I left after lunch on Friday the 15th and made the drive to the hotel alone. Of course, I called Daddy as soon as I got there. He was nervous, to say the least.

Since we had our car, I picked Lee J. up from the base around 8 am. We went back to the hotel and spent most of the day there. This was in August. It was so hot, so the pool was a big attraction for us. I look at the hairdo I had in the pool pictures we made, and I'm amazed at the styles of the day. Lee J. always said he liked it. He called it "Hair jacked up to Jesus."

We spent a lot of time talking about his graduation in three weeks. He didn't have his assignment yet, but he was pretty sure we would be going to Sheppard AFB in Wichita Falls, Texas. As it turned out, that's what happened. He was excited because it was an all-jet program with no T-41s. I wanted it, too, because Wichita Falls was less than 3 hours back to Idalou. Before he left for OTS, during an inspection of the T-41 program, he'd met an officer stationed at Randolph AFB. The guy had a friend who worked in assignments. He got Lee J.'s orders to Sheppard AFB set up before OTS even started. It was another example of the old adage, "It's not what you know, but who you know."

We went back to the River Walk late Saturday afternoon and enjoyed the atmosphere once more with some great Mexican food. This time, we took one of the tour boats and saw a lot more of the River Walk than we did four weeks earlier. We didn't stay very long after the boat ride was over. I think we both were ready to get back to the hotel. Lee J. has said for years that nights with me in a hotel/motel room are, at the very least, quite interesting and, at the most, incredible. That night was one of the incredible ones. It was comforting to know that I only had to endure three more weeks with Mother and Daddy. After that, Lee J. and I would be spending every night together once again. I loved lying in his arms; with him, my world was complete.

We spent Sunday hanging out at the hotel and the pool. Since I had the car and was not going to drive home in the dark, I would spend another night at the hotel. The base had some pretty ratty VOQ rooms we could use. He could sign in on base at 5 pm, and we could have a room until he had to be back at the barracks at 10 pm. So, I got to stay with him for another five hours. We drove to the base, and he signed in. We then went over to the VOQ office. They didn't have much available, but we took what they had. It turns out that the A/C was hardly working in the room we got, and that room was **hot**. He asked me if I really wanted to stay, and I said, "Absolutely!"

We left what little stuff we'd brought in the room and headed over to the OT club. It was both air-conditioned and nearby. There were a few singles and some couples, but it was pretty dead. We decided to get some food and kill a little time before returning to the sweatbox—VOQ room. The A/C worked a little, but not nearly enough. We decided the only way to stay anywhere close to cool was to take our clothes off and push the bed close to the window A/C unit. So that's what we did. What a sight we must have made. We were naked as jaybirds as we lay there and laughed at our situation. That room must have been 95 degrees at least.

I don't remember which one of us said something to the effect that we had come to the VOQ, knowing full well we planned to make love one more time before we had to leave each other again. No preparation was required since we were both already naked, so that's what we did. I remember us giggling a lot, but soon, we were both really into it. Maybe sweat is an aphrodisiac; something must have been because our lovemaking was both sweaty and fabulous. Afterwards, we lay on the bed to catch our breath, sweat pouring off both of us, and my hair was a wreck. I was sure I looked awful. We got up and showered together but didn't put our clothes back on. The shower had cooled us off somewhat, but that room was still hot. Finally, it was time; we had to get ready to leave. I was sure glad I'd brought an extra change of clothes; I needed them. What a memory we'd made with our time in that sweatbox of a room in the Lackland VOQ! We've never forgotten that experience, and as I was writing this, we both had a good laugh about it once again. It was gross; we were gross, but it **was fun!**

I took Lee J. back to his barracks at about 10 pm, and then we had to say goodbye once more. Of course, we both were quite sad, but not as much as the time before. It had been a memorable two days, and the end of the separation was in sight. I remember giving him a deep, memorable goodbye kiss, and then he watched as I drove away. I went back to the hotel for what was to be a very lonely night. I drove home the next day. Daddy was happy to see me safely home; his chickens were all back in the roost.

The routine began again, except I had given notice that Friday, August 29, would be my last day at Travelers. I only had to endure two more weeks. Raymond and Gwen were going to the graduation and suggested we drive down together. The kids would be going, too. We would take two cars and drive down on Thursday before his graduation on Friday. We planned to spend Thursday and Friday night and then drive home on Saturday, and that's what we did.

When we got to the hotel on Thursday, we got all checked in. Lee J. could leave the base, so I left to pick him up. We returned to the hotel, and he had a great reunion with the kids and his folks. They couldn't get over how much weight he had put on. He left weighing 150 pounds and now weighed 175; I thought he looked great.

As we all were sitting around the pool with Granny Gwen and Pa-Pa Raymond watching the kids play in the water, Gwen did one of the sweetest things ever. Out of nowhere, she suggested that Lee J. and I could probably use a little time to "rest." She said, "Y'all go on to your room, and we'll take care of the kids for a couple of hours."

Let's just say we didn't get a lot of rest in those two hours. When we got to our room, we both laughed at how my mother-in-law had told us **in code** to go get our sexual needs taken care of, and so we did. I learned a lot about my mother-in-law that day. However, for the moment, we needed each other desperately again. We lost ourselves once more as we used the entire two hours to the fullest. When we emerged from our room, I had an appreciation for my mother-in-law I'd never known before. To this day, I remember that gesture from her as a very sweet memory. She obviously knew the kind of "rest" we needed.

We went down to the River Walk that night. His folks had never been there before, and they thought it was really something special. It wasn't quite the same as it had been earlier for me since our kids and his folks were with us, but that was just fine. The next day was his military graduation and I was to become an Air Force officer's wife. There was a lot of marching by the graduates and the Lackland AFB band. It was quite the spectacle for Lee J.'s dad, especially. I could tell he was so proud of his son. I was, too. After it was over, we went by the barracks and picked up his stuff. He signed out for the last time. OTS was over! We drove home the next day, and Lee J. had a great reunion with my family.

So, what was my takeaway from what I still think of as the worst three months of my life? Separation from my husband leaves a hole in me that is hard to endure. But as miserable as it was, I learned that if I must, I can endure something like this; I can still function as a mom while holding a job and being good at it. One of the big things I learned was that under the right circumstances, I could find ways to release things I had bottled up inside me.

During those first weeks of separation, I suppressed an enormous amount of emotion deep within me. I never complained to anyone (especially Mother) about the way I felt. I did what I'd learned to do as a child; I contained all those emotions within myself. So, I had a lot going on just beneath the surface when I got to San Antonio that first time. I found a release through the lovemaking with Lee J. He certainly didn't understand exactly what had happened in the hotel room that morning until much later. Actually, I didn't understand either.

I would find that during the next five years, our time in the Air Force, I would again experience times when I could unburden myself from a lot of pent-up emotional baggage dating all the way back to my childhood. I found release through the great relationship (both sexual and nonsexual) I had with my wonderful husband and the feeling of freedom that came simply from being far away from home. However, what I went through during those three months was a hard way to get an education. But I did come away from those OTS months as a much stronger person.

After a day or two back in Idalou, Lee J. and I headed to Wichita Falls to get started on the next phase of our military adventure. We found a house to rent, and he signed in, though he was still on leave. He was to report officially in about a week. He was excited because now the flying would begin, and I was excited because we were together once more. We both were beyond happy.

INTO THE WILD BLUE YONDER

Well into the T-38 phase, when the guys were night flying, for whatever reason, Angie decided to push four butter beans up her nose. I discovered what she had done and figured out I couldn't remove them. I knew Lee J. wouldn't be home until the early morning hours, so I loaded up both kids and headed to the ER at the base. I didn't think the people there were very friendly, but they took some special scissor/tweezer-like things and got the beans out. I was a frazzled wreck, but I had taken care of the "crisis." Angie was fine, but I still have no idea what possessed her to stuff beans up her nose. (Lee J. always called her our "space cadet.") When he came in at about four in the morning, I told him what had happened. At first, he thought it was kind of funny, but he soon could tell I found little humor in the whole episode. He then complimented me on handling it. The scenario taught me that I could handle crises far better than I had ever imagined. That would come in handy again soon enough.

Not long after the beans-in-the-nose episode, another medical issue emerged. We had been to a squadron-wide picnic on a Saturday when Angie was playing with some other kids on the slide. Somehow, she fell off the ladder and hurt her arm. We didn't think it was hurt very badly, and after the picnic, we took her home. She kept whining for a couple of days, so I finally took her to the ER on Tuesday. Of course, Lee J. was not home, so I again went to the ER with both kids in tow to have her checked out. Again, they weren't terribly friendly and didn't think it was broken. But when the X-Rays came back, sure enough, the poor kid had a broken arm. I felt so bad about not getting her checked out earlier, but we got her fixed up. Once more, I was forced to handle a situation by myself. I was amazed at what I could do if I had to.

I was learning to handle things that I'd never been expected to do before we joined the Air Force. I found that I was no longer intimidated by facing something new. Of course, my anxiety ramped up a bit, but I was far more confident that I could handle the unexpected if I had to. It actually gave me a good feeling. I would find that the longer we were in the military, the more things I would be responsible for, I was becoming okay with that.

As I've previously written, I had not enjoyed our first months as a military family, but that was soon to change. The house we rented in Wichita Falls was just perfect for us. It had three bedrooms, which let the kids have a playroom. There was a huge carport with an extra storage room behind that and a small yard. Moving wasn't a big chore since the Air Force had stored our stuff while OTS was going on. We notified the proper people, and they showed up with our furniture and even set it all up. Basically, we moved in and were pretty well settled in one day.

Lee J. was quickly involved with all the new guy

orientation things a new pilot trainee had to go through. He was one happy camper as were his wife and two kids. At last, we were sleeping in our own bed. I could snuggle down with my husband for the night, occasionally awakened by a couple of little urchins who would pile in with us in the mornings. After a three-month separation and a little time to get settled in our new home, I finally found my happy place, and I loved it.

I won't spend a lot of time talking about how Lee J.'s training would go. Suffice it to say, he was planning on being number one, and that's exactly the way it was going. For the first time in our marriage, we had a social life. There was something going on almost every weekend, involving some of the other guys in his class. We'd made friends with the Alons, Dwayne and Clairice, who lived on base. They were from Iowa and off a farm. He and Lee J. had a lot in common, and they would end up competing for the top spot at the end of training. They had two little boys about the same age as Julie and Angie. We spent time with them as the guys studied together. It was such a treat for me to have someone like Clairice to talk to. I hadn't had that since high school.

Our other friendship developed with Chuck and Anna Miller. They had gotten married during the Christmas break and lived close by. Chuck also came from a farm background. We saw them a lot after Christmas. I even learned how to play spades at their house, though I was never very good at it. They loved our kids, and the kids loved to be around them, too.

One of the best things about the whole situation was that

Lee J.'s salary and benefits were going to be more than adequate to meet our financial needs. I wasn't going to have to work outside the home. I was able to be a stay-at-home mom, and I loved it. He used to call this situation "living-the-dream." For the first time ever, I was "living-my-dream."

Life for me and the girls could not have been better. By now, Lee J. had realized that he was meant to be the dad of girls (little girls especially, teenagers maybe not so much). Being married to him when he was doing something he genuinely loved to do was a totally different experience for me than what I had known at times earlier in our marriage. I'm quite sure the same is true for him, too. Coming home to me and those little girls always seemed to be a treat for him. The kids grew to really love their daddy, and I didn't care at all that they both had him wrapped around their little fingers.

The only downside for me was my anxiety would ramp up whenever a big check ride or academic test for him was coming. He used to kid me and say that I could be the "designated worrier" for our family, so I guess I filled that role. We began our ritual when he would come home after a check ride or an academic test. I would meet him as he came home and immediately solemnly ask, "How did it go?" I always feigned relief when he gave me the results (which were generally excellent). I would then give him a very passionate kiss. I'd learned that a passionate kiss was a good way to send a message to him in "code." (This goes back to the way I'd learned to tease him on our honeymoon.)

He would then tentatively ask me, "Does the kiss you just

gave me mean that I **have to take a second "check ride"** later tonight?"

I would lower my head and eyes and solemnly tell him, "Yes, that's exactly what it means!"

It doesn't take much imagination to figure out what kind of "check ride" I was going to give him later that night. He used to laugh and say the second "check ride" he took with me was a lot more fun than the first one of the day. Also, he would tell me that I was a far prettier check "airperson" than the first one of the day, too. Of course, I administered his "check ride" sans a flight suit. Let's just say that on those check rides, I did the "riding." I'll offer no more explanation than that. He generally got "excellent" grades on the second check ride, too. **What fun! How I did love my guy!**

It seemed needless to worry, for he was cruising along with his training, especially in the T-37 phase. He hid his anxiety well from me, but he did have some. A lot was riding on his class standing, which determined his assignment out of pilot training. But everything basically went off without a hitch.

Our personal relationship had never been better. He told me he now knew that he was born to fly airplanes and how much he loved it. Also, he was even more sure that he was born to be married to me. How I loved to hear him say that. Our passion for each other had always been high, but it was off the charts again now. All this carried over to him with the kids. Those girls adored their daddy, and their favorite game with him was to play dog pile on him when he was relaxing

134

on the couch.

We soon figured out that a second mode of transportation would be nice. An interesting story develops from that need. It also paints a picture of the guy I was married to; he loved being "different." Lee J. had to fill me in on some of the details about all this, but I think I got most of this right.

The first time we went home after moving to Wichita Falls, Lee J. saw one of his daddy's old pickup trucks, a 1958, **worn out,** yellow and white Ford pickup, sitting derelict by their yard. He asked his dad if it would run. Raymond told him it was running when he parked it there several months before. Lee J. asked him if he got it running, would he sell it to him. Raymond said he would. He then asked him what he would take for it. Raymond said, "One dollar!" Lee J. asked him if he would take a check, and his dad said no, he wanted cash. They got it running, bought a green hood from a junkyard for it, and somehow got it inspected. All this was done on a Saturday while we were there. I just thought the old Desoto I had to drive in Amarillo was awful. This contraption made the Desoto look like something off the showroom floor.

He also saw an old tractor tire and had his dad throw it in as part of the $1 pickup purchase. It was to be a sandbox for Raymond's granddaughters. We headed for Wichita Falls the next day, and it got there amidst the smoke and all. Lee J. said it used a "little" oil. There would be many tales to talk about concerning that old truck. Suffice it to say, the ridicule Lee J. endured from his classmates just made it that much more fun for him. His German classmates couldn't believe any self-respecting pilot would be seen in anything quite that ugly. His carpool guys weren't all that thrilled about their chariot, either. He said they particularly weren't fond of the continual "smoke in the cockpit."

When we got home with it, it had become a three-tone truck. It was originally a two-toned yellow and white, but the added junkyard hood was green. It was hideous! He decided to paint it with a brush. He bought a gallon of blue paint, and the next Saturday, I watched from the window as his three-toned truck became simply bright blue. It still was hideous! The derision from his classmates knew no bounds. He put some Chevrolet hubcaps on it and called it all good. There is just something about him that doesn't mind being the butt of his friends' jokes. I think it comes from his supreme confidence in himself and the fact that he was number one in the class. He absolutely loved driving that piece of junk. I think you get the picture that my husband liked being the "class clown."

The next Saturday after the paint job, we decided to make a trip up to the Red River north of Wichita Falls to procure some sand for the tractor tire sandbox in our backyard. We found just the right spot on a sandbar by the river, and he let the kids "help" him put the sand in the back of the pickup. We got back home with it, and soon, the girls were doing their thing in the sandpile. Our whole household was "living the dream."

As the pilot training year really got into high gear after

everyone had soloed out in the T-37 program, the girls and I got into a routine. They were old enough not to need my constant undivided attention. We got them a swing set for the backyard to go with their custom sandbox, so they were outside a lot. I started sewing again and kept us in some new clothes. I was really enjoying myself. We probably made three trips home before Christmas. One was to go to Kathy's wedding. She had met a guy, Chuck Flusche, and they married in November, eleven months after Karla was born. There was not so much drama now at Mother's when we went home.

The Air Force shut down pilot training for two weeks over Christmas, so we had a fun Christmas break that we spent with everyone back in Idalou. Lee J. had tried to get his blue pickup home for Christmas. He planned to overhaul the motor, which was going to be his Christmas present from Raymond and Gwen. The pickup didn't make it. It threw a rod outside of Seymore, but my southern engineering husband rigged a towing system from the chains on the tailgate and latched it to our car. I drove the car with the kids and me while slowly towing him, driving his junker all the way to Idalou. I was not a happy camper, but he was right; we didn't have any other choice. I think it took four hours to drag it from Seymore to Idalou. I was embarrassed, while he thought it was funny. Maybe it was funny since we've had some good laughs out of it over the years.

Over the holidays, he overhauled the engine and put some good tires on it, making it more reliable. Raymond kidded him, saying he thought he might want it back now; he didn't get it. Christmas at home was good, and everyone could tell we were just fine. When it was time to go back, I was relieved that I wasn't towing him again, and we made it back just fine. Even Ken and Chuck, his carpoolers, thought it was an improvement. At least now, there was no smoke in the cockpit.

It was back to work now after the holidays and to finish off the T-37 phase. Lee J. did well and maintained his first position in the class. My life became pretty idyllic. I was with my girls all the time; my husband was home almost every night; we had a good social life with some of his classmates. I really couldn't ask for much more. Still, I did have some anxiety whenever he had a big test or check ride, but then again, that was part of my job as the family's "designated worrier." The T-37 phase was over in late March. Lee J. said the real fun would begin when they went to the T-38s. He was still number one and was halfway through the program. He was happy.

The T-38 phase would be a bit more pressure-packed because he no longer had an edge over the rest of the guys due to his previous experience. There's nothing in the civilian aviation world to compare with the "38." He loved flying that airplane and did it very well. During this phase, I had a couple of experiences that I'll never forget. The narrative at the start of this chapter describes them.

As Lee J.'s UPT class approached graduation day, October 24, 1970, things had gone pretty much as he had planned. He did not graduate number one, but he was number one when their dream sheets went in. He got the assignment of his choice, an F-106, but It would not have made any difference anyway since he and Dwayne weren't vying for the same assignment.

I should explain a little about Lee J.'s assignment. As I related earlier, his initial desire, when he talked to me about "us" joining the Air Force, was to get an assignment flying big airplanes such as the C-141, the KC-135, and such. However, at the last instance, he'd had a change of heart that caused him a bit of consternation when filling out his "dream sheet." When he started the T-38 training phase, each student pilot had a "dollar ride" in which the instructor showed them what the "38" could do. Lee J. told me it was an eye-opening experience. The following is a passage I copied from his autobiography that explains things in his own words.

"On June 5, 1970, I had my first front seat ride in the "38." Captain Dampman, who was to be my regular instructor for the entire "38" program, was my instructor that day. This introductory ride in the front seat was called the "dollar ride," because every instructor bet his student one dollar that he could not roll less than 360 degrees with a quick full stick deflection of the ailerons. The instructors never lost that bet. I don't think it is humanly possible to fully deflect the stick in a "38" and not roll more than 360 degrees. About the best anyone could do was a full roll plus ninety degrees. That means the wings were perpendicular to the horizon instead of being the normal parallel to the horizon. It was mind-boggling and disorienting.

The reason I called this ride life changing was because I had promised

*Sandy I would choose a transport type assignment for my Air Force career. After losing the bet to Capt. Dampman, doing a Mach run (went supersonic), performing some aerobatics, I was losing all interest in flying transport type aircraft. The icing on the cake was when Capt. Dampman asked me if I wanted to see what it was like to simulate strafing (shooting a gun at) a bridge. Of course, I said, "Yes!!!!" Capt. Dampman came to Sheppard after flying F-4's, and he was a true fighter pilot at heart. We picked out a small bridge on the highway between Seymore, Texas, and the Sheppard AFB traffic pattern. He showed me how to roll in on the bridge and then we "shot the hell out of it," followed by a four-g pull-off. From that moment on, I never wanted to fly transports again. **I wanted to fly some kind of fighter!** I didn't tell Sandy! I had created a problem for myself, and I truly didn't know how I was going to handle it. For the time being, I said nothing to Sandy."*

Lee J.'s problem was that as number one in the class, he could have his choice of assignments. He never told me that he was thinking about a fighter assignment. He truly didn't know what he was going to do. The following is also from his autobiography, which explains how he worked out his assignment problem and kept his promise of a "safe" assignment to me. A better word would be a "safer" assignment because the F-106 could be a very dangerous airplane to fly.

"About a week before we were to fill out our dream sheets, I was at the officer's club one Friday afternoon for an officer's call, and one of the senior instructors tapped me on the shoulder and motioned me to come to a table away from the rest of my classmates. For the second time during

pilot training, I had an encounter that would change my life. (The first was the "dollar" ride with Capt. Dampman.)

Major Hennig was well known in the squadron as a straight shooter type of guy, but I had no idea what he wanted to talk to me about. He grinned and said, "Lt. you've got a problem, don't you?"

I'm sure I looked puzzled and said, "I'm not sure what you're asking about?"

He then said, "You've promised your wife that you would take a "many-motor" (transport or such) assignment out of pilot training, and now you want to fly a fighter." (I'm not sure how he knew about that, but some of my classmates knew of my dilemma and one of them obviously had said something.)

I told him, "That's right, and I do have a problem."

He said, "I'm going to give you a little advice and you can take it or leave it."

I said, "Okay."

He then gave me his thoughts. He said, "What we're doing in Vietnam is wrong! We're not fighting to win over there. I've had too many friends that either got shot down and died or were captured and are now in the Hanoi Hilton. What a waste! We're taught to fight to win, but that's not what we're doing." He went on to say, "You've got a beautiful young wife and two little girls that you need to take care of. You have an option you may not have thought about. If I were you, I'd try to get an ADC (Air Defense Command) assignment as opposed to a TAC (Tactical Air Command) assignment. For the most part, they are all located stateside.

Try to get an F-106, F-102, or F-101 assignment. You'll love the flying, and you'll be stationed accompanied by your family. Think about it!" I did and a week later I filled out my dream sheet just like he suggested. It turned out to be a great piece of advice. I went home and told Sandy what Maj. Hennig had said, and as long as we could stay together, she was fine with it. It would turn out that way."

It had been quite a year for both of us. I was happy in every way. He would achieve his goal of a choice assignment, but most importantly, it was an assignment that would allow us to be together for the next several years. I had become a very competent young officer's wife, and I was proud of us both. The big thing was that the pressure was off. We were now in the real Air Force. He still had advanced training to do, but he was now a rated pilot. That was a big deal. I pinned his wings on him at the graduation ceremony and we began a new phase in our lives, our marriage, and his career as a pilot.

He had been able to keep his promise to me and also fulfill his dream of a fighter assignment. Sometimes, things just work out. He was assigned to fly the F-106. He will tell you it turned out to be a dream come true. My only thought was that it was a really beautiful airplane. If he was happy with the assignment, then I would be too. But little did I know that we would soon spend four months in Florida, where he would learn to fly the "6." It would be during those months that I would begin to experience some deep psychological changes in myself.

But before that, we would have a short detour to Perrin AFB in Sherman, Texas. Originally, he was to be there for some lead-in training in the F-102 before going to Florida for training in the F-106. It was to be four months. However, he got caught in a time when the Air Force was changing the way they would train new F-106 pilots. We ended up in Sherman with him doing essentially nothing but working on his old blue truck. He did fly about thirty hours in the T-33, which he hated. We would get to Florida around the end of March 1971 for his F-106 training. So it was to be a life on the beach we'd never dreamed of before.

Sun on My Skin, Sand Between My Toes

We'd been in Florida about a month when the first of our guests from West Texas arrived. It was Lee J.'s mother and dad, along with his aunt Lela and uncle T.B. They had a great time, but the following description from Lee J.'s autobiography turned out to be the high point of their stay for his dad.

"The biggest event of their stay turned out to be a surprise for me as well as for them. It seems that they were staying with us during the weekend when General Price (the Commanding General of Tyndall AFB) had one of his periodic revues of his troops and the aircraft that were a part of Tyndall's overall mission. I had heard about it and asked all our guests if they would like to go. They all said yes; so, we went.

It was held on Saturday, so we all loaded up and headed to the parade grounds which were adjacent to the flight line. We were seated in bleachers behind the reviewing stand. The troops marched in review while the band played. Exactly at a predetermined moment in the playing of the National Anthem, there were sixteen aircraft directly overhead in formation for a flyby. It was not your normal flyby. There were four four-ship diamond formations flying together as a single sixteen-ship diamond formation. It was impressive.

Shortly after the sixteen-ship diamond formation passed, they reformed into four echelon formations with each following the other with about a sixteen second interval between formations. The sixteen-ship flyby had come from our right to our left. The echelon formations returned from our left to our right. They started their pitch outs overhead using four second interval spacing. As the last ship in the formation ahead pitched, four seconds later the first aircraft in the next formation pitched, and so on until all the aircraft were in the landing pattern or were taxiing in. After landing they all kept their spacing and one by one they all taxied in and parked line abreast along the flightline in front of us. The ones directly in front of where we were seated were no more than thirty yards away.

After the last aircraft had taxied in there were sixteen fighter jets all lined abreast with engines still running some directly in front of us. A signal was given, and all the aircraft shutdown in unison; then simultaneously all the canopies opened in unison; crew chiefs walked to the aircraft and hung the ladders in unison; the pilots all stood and exited their cockpits in unison; they then all took a few steps forward and salutes were exchanged between the pilots and the crew chiefs in unison. Then from each end, the pilots started marching toward the reviewing stand, and then they all saluted General Price in unison.

It had been one helluva show; It had been beautiful; it had been loud; it had been impressive. I was seated next to Daddy during all this and he seemed mesmerized. I'm sure he had never witnessed anything quite like this, for that matter, nor had I. After the last salute and everything was over, he turned to me and in a kind of question he said, "They're teaching

145

you to fly these airplanes and do all this kind of stuff?"

I just nodded and replied, "Yeah they are!"

His only reply as he shook his head was an unbelieving, "Damn!"

I think for the first time he realized just what I was involved in and what I was so passionate about. I learned later that when he got back home, he drove his friends that hung around the gin office crazy with his description of all the stuff I was involved in. He was starting to realize just what I was learning to do."

Lee J. had always desired his dad's approval for the things he did, and Raymond was certainly proud of his accomplishments. However, he didn't think his dad really had a grasp on just what his training to become a fighter pilot entailed; for that matter, initially, neither did I. The show we had just witnessed that morning was an eye-opener for both his dad and myself. It was really impressive.

Our time in Florida has to be one of the high points in my life and Lee J.'s, too. We were a couple of West Texas kids who never saw the beach unless it was on a vacation. Looking back on our four months in Florida in 1971, it was a four-month vacation, especially for the kids and me. Lee J. was getting checked out (trained) in the F-106, so he was "working," but he would hardly call it that. He was literally having the time of his life while learning to fly the "6" and also when he was at the beach house with us. So, how did all of this come about?

We arrived at Tyndall AFB in late March of 1971. Lee J. checked in at the base, and while talking with some of the people stationed there, they told him that a lot of the TDY (Temporary Duty) people rented houses at Mexico Beach. It was a small resort town about 10 miles down the road from the base. So, that's where we headed. We stopped at a real estate/rental office and inquired about a place we could rent for four months. They showed us the beach house. It was in our price range and only about a block off the beach. It was not posh by any standard, but we liked it and signed a four-month rental agreement. Our adventure began.

We were allowed 600 pounds of household goods that had been shipped from Sherman, and we had it all delivered ASAP. One of the things that I had included in the 600 pounds was my sewing machine. Little did I know how much I would use it during our stay at Mexico Beach. We had a few days before Lee J. started his training. So, we took advantage of that time and explored all the things available to us. I was like a kid in a candy store. This was so different from anything I'd ever experienced. The house had two bedrooms with a large kitchen and living area, but it had an extra room on the back that had six double bunk beds. Little did we know how much that extra room would get used.

Within a day or so after our arrival, I soon figured out that I would have to modify the way I'd normally worn my hair. "Hair jacked up to Jesus" was not going to work as my beach "do." I told him that it was actually quite liberating to be able to just brush my hair and put a hair band in it. He told me he thought I looked more beautiful than ever when I modeled my new beach "do" for him. Personally, I was glad I wasn't going to have to spend a great deal of time fixing and worrying about my hair.

The other thing I told him was that the clothes I'd been wearing in Texas were not going to work very well as beach attire for our summer in Florida. I wanted us to go back into Panama City and just drive around, so we did. I was looking to see what others similar to myself were wearing. Before leaving Panama City, we stopped by a fabric store, and I bought some fabrics for me to start working on. I told Lee J. that it appeared that anything and everything was being worn, and I could wear whatever I felt comfortable in and not feel out of place.

I soon decided something simple and cool was going to be my attire of choice. I asked Lee J. to help me design an easy-to-make halter top that I could quickly sew for myself. He helped me make a pattern out of some newspapers. I already had a pattern for some shorts that I liked, which were simple to make. To be quite honest, I thought I had a figure that was perfect for the minimal, casual look that I had seen in Panama City.

Going without a bra was totally in fashion; shorts and halters were common for young women my age, as I saw as we looked around that day. Even though I'd had two kids, my breasts were still quite firm. Lee J.'s word for them was "perky," so I was extremely comfortable wearing tops that didn't require a bra. That soon became my favorite way to be and would be for years to come. We soon produced an amazingly uncomplicated halter design that I thought looked really good on me.

As I related earlier, my sewing machine was included in our six hundred pounds of TDY household goods and I got it out when our stuff was delivered a couple of days later. I went right to work on my first project. The kids and I would soon have matching outfits that were eye-catching. Lee J. started calling us his "eye candy." Though he may have been somewhat prejudiced, I liked it when he said things like that about his girls. I even had one lady stop me and ask where I'd bought our matching outfits. She was disappointed when I told her I'd made them all myself. I don't remember how many outfits I made that summer, but there were several.

Looking back now, I soon started to realize that I was 1,100 miles from home. All the old rules I had grown up adhering to no longer applied to me if I chose to do more of my own thing. **So, I did.** I think my choice of attire was one way to be both comfortable in a beach environment and also feel free to push aside the mores of my upbringing in Idalou. I was starting to feel the stirring of an underlying freedom similar to what I'd felt on our honeymoon.

We had been in Mexico Beach for about a month when Lee J.'s parents, along with his aunt Lela and uncle T.B., arrived for a 5 or 6-day visit. His aunt had hardly ever been out of Van Zandt County in Texas, let alone to Florida. I don't think I've ever seen anyone so happy and complimentary to me for the hospitality we showed them. T.B. and Raymond spent a lot of their time on the fishing pier. Of course, Raymond never met a stranger, and they had a great time fishing. I'm not sure they ever caught anything, but to hear them tell it, they had an entertaining time with the others who were fishing there too. I spent a lot of time cooking and making sandwiches for everyone, but I enjoyed every minute of it.

Before they arrived, I was a little worried that my normal attire might not be appropriate for me to wear in front of our guests. As I've related earlier, all I wore was shorts, halters, and small bikini swimwear. Lee J. told me that I had nothing to worry about, and I didn't. In fact, the first time we all went down to the beach together, the kids and I all wore our normal swimsuits. Lee J.'s mother and his aunt had their pant legs rolled up so they could wade in the shallow surf. I wore my little blue bikini that covered me just enough. When I removed my coverup, Aunt Lela told me how beautiful she thought I looked. That statement totally eased my mind. She was one of the kindest and sweetest people ever. They stayed with us for almost a week, and I think we all enjoyed it immensely. Of course, it was during this time we saw the events described at the beginning of this chapter. Raymond went back home with a lot to tell about Lee J. and his Air Force adventures. He was so proud of his son but also of me and the girls too.

Lee J.'s training was really going well. He was having the time of his life. The kids and I were too. It was that summer in Florida when I had the opportunity, like never before, to lay out. The kids and I generally went to the beach in the late morning. While the kids played in the sand, I would lay on a small raft in the shallows. I loved it. If Lee J. was on the morning schedule, he told me he generally could see me and the kids at the beach every time they turned on the ten-mile final for the traffic pattern at Tyndall. Even from a 1500' altitude, he said it was easy to see us. He even pointed us out to his instructor, whom I would soon get a chance to meet.

Of course, he didn't have the same opportunity to go to the beach as the girls and I did, but after he'd finished most of the academic portion of his training, he would get some half days off. When that happened, all four of us would head to the beach together. When he was around, I really got into sunning. We had found a semi-secluded spot to sunbathe back against the sand dunes on the far side of the waterway on the west side of town. I would have him undo my top when I laid on my stomach, and when I rolled over on my back, I would just lay my top on me unfastened. It was barely there. As the summer wore on, I became increasingly daring and finally started sunbathing without my top at all since we seldom saw anyone on that beach.

I tell all of this because I was feeling something just beneath the surface that I **needed** to express. I've alluded to some of my feelings earlier in these writings, but it was that summer in Florida when I first talked to Lee J. about how I felt. I told him I wanted to free myself from the shy, bashful girl I once was and become someone who had more of a "free spirit." He thought my somewhat daring sunbathing was a part of these feelings, and it probably was. However, when I was around others, I never did anything remotely inappropriate. He was somewhat puzzled by what I was saying and doing, but he absolutely loved who I was becoming.

Lee J.'s instructor in the "6" was a great guy named Larry Livingston. He was married and had a couple of little boys about the girls' age. One weekend, fairly early in Lee J.'s training, Larry invited us to go out with them on their boat. We took him up on the invitation. I'd never met him before the excursion that day, but both he and his wife were very comfortable to be around. Our girls played well with their boys. They took us to a small island where we could let the kids play in the sand and shallow water while we sat on the beach and talked; I really liked his wife. The guys ended up talking about flying, and his wife and I were just two moms enjoying each other's company.

We went out with them on their boat a couple more times during our stay. I'll always remember he started teasing me about how dark my tan was and gave me a nickname. He started calling me Gomez. There was nothing untoward about his comments, and I guess I liked his attention. As I've previously stated, Lee J. was telling me that the girls and I were turning heads wherever we went. (I'm sure it was the "matchy, matchy" outfits.) He told me quite often that summer, every guy likes to have some "eye candy" with him. He said that few get the triple dose that he had. I did love it when he said things like that.

As his training was changing him, I was changing, too (more about that later). He was in awe of his situation. We thought back to the time, when he initially approached me about joining the Air Force, we could have never dreamed of the scenario we were now living in. He was learning to fly, as he called it, one helluva airplane. According to his training debriefs, he was not only doing satisfactorily; he was getting excellent reviews from the instructors. The camaraderie of being around a bunch of fighter pilots was like nothing he had ever experienced before. His passion for what he was engaged in left him exhilarated.

It was an all-male, fighter pilots filled environment in which he was immersed daily at the base and a very girly household that he came home to later. He was married to what he said was the most beautiful, passionate woman any man could ever want, plus there were the two little girls who really loved their daddy. I knew he felt immense pride and satisfaction being with us. Lee J. and I both found ourselves being beyond happy. When you add the passion he had for me and the kids to the passion he felt for what he was learning to do, he told me that never before had he felt so complete. The beauty of it all was that we still had June and July to go.

Sometime in late May, we had another "horde" of West Texans descending upon us. This time, it was Mother, Daddy, Barb, Dan, and their kids. It was another blast. Mother loved to travel, and she was really loving this trip. Of course, the kids wanted to spend as much time on the beach as possible; we did. Lee J. had to "work," so like I'd done when his folks visited earlier, I helped them explore some of the sights in the area. The kids had their cousins, Kristi and Steve, to play with on the beach, and we all spent an enormous amount of time there. I've sometimes wondered what Mother thought about my new choices in attire that I wore while they were there. She never said a word, and I'm sure she was fine with it; after all, I was living on the beach. They all seemed to have a great time, but after nearly a week, they too had to leave. It was back to our regular routine.

Mid-June, we had some more company from West Texas. Earl Swinford, his wife, and son were coming to Florida on vacation, and he'd learned we were living there for the summer. He called and asked if they could come by. We told them they were certainly welcome, not only to come by but to stay with us for a while. Earl had been Lee J.'s guitar teacher and employer in years gone by. They stayed three days and then went on to their original destination. He gave Lee J. a guitar in exchange for our hospitality. Lee J. still has that guitar today.

We had more visitors from West Texas when Joe and Brenda, my sister, stopped by for the night shortly after the Swinfords left. They were on their way to see Joe's brother, Tom, in central Florida. They would be the last of our West Texas visitors.

In late June, we knew our time at the Mexico Beach house would be drawing to a close at the end of the next month. There would be no more West Texas visitors, but we were still in full vacation mode. As much as we enjoyed having our company visit us, we also enjoyed our time together as a family. Lee J. loved his girls, and I'm including myself in that scenario. In talking with each other about the writing of my experiences in Florida, I think we discovered some things about me that were a bit surprising to both of us. At about this time during our Florida stay, I started to let my inner feelings emerge. He was seeing a new side of me on a consistent basis.

The four months in Florida were a very sensory-loaded time for us. Lee J. was experiencing becoming a part of an elite fighter pilot community. Fighter squadrons in those days were a male-only environment. To say it was a testosterone-loaded situation would be an understatement. He was being taught to fly an airplane whose mission was to fight! Being aggressive, confident, and a bit cocky were all in the daily equation for him. No, he didn't come home ready to fight, far from it, but he did come home to a house full of girls he loved. He told me repeatedly we had the cutest kids ever and I was the hottest thing he had ever seen. I made no effort to correct him.

On the other hand, I was 1,100 miles from home in a very sensory-loaded environment for me, too. I had always loved being outdoors, and now I had the opportunity to spend my days on the beach in nothing but a very revealing bikini. A short time after we arrived there, I had the best tan of my life. As I mentioned earlier, Larry, Lee J.'s "106" instructor, nicknamed me Gomez because my tan was so dark, probably too dark, but it was what it was. I was becoming more and more aware that the girls and I turned heads almost anywhere, but especially on the beach. I'll admit there was a part of me that loved the attention.

To be quite honest, I'd never considered myself to be one who was excessively vain. I always thought I looked okay. However, my husband told me over and over that I was the sexiest, most beautiful woman he'd ever seen. As dumb as he was as a young man, he had learned that my love language, "words of affirmation," was something that was very real to me. I suppose I'd started to believe him. That summer, I'd become tanned, toned, and completely comfortable wearing some very skimpy swimwear. I'm sure some of the inner stirrings and feelings I was experiencing had something to do with the new confidence I felt about my looks. Looking back now, I realize I was in the process of throwing off one of my mother's mantras about not "tooting my own horn." I now thought I looked great. **There, I said it!**

I now knew that the entire time we'd lived at Mexico Beach, there was an inner part of me I was in the process of discovering. I loved the freedom the beach gave me to push my shyness aside and let an alter ego start to emerge. The opening scene of this book was set in late June during a Saturday beach picnic we had. I won't recount the entire scene, but to better understand all of this, rereading that part might be helpful. That day on that secluded beach, I let what I was feeling inside me become who I **was.** Who I **was** that day was a far cry from who I had been up to that point in my life. (I'm calling a timeout here.)

I'm inserting these next five paragraphs to help explain what was going on inside me that day. I think by explaining the psychology of what I was feeling and where it came from should give a better understanding of my actions on that day. It also explains my similar behavior for days and even years to come. So here goes!

What was causing all the feelings I was having? Though I'm not a psychologist, I've read an enormous amount about how suppressed childhood emotions can build up and affect us later in life. (**I've experienced some of that.**) I grew up not expressing many of my emotions. I suppressed them. I also grew up with some pretty strict rules about how I should behave. One of the articles I found really struck a chord with me. Its focus was on "taking rules applied to us as children and unnecessarily carrying them subconsciously into adulthood ." (**I believe that I did that.**)

Several questions were posed for the reader to answer. "Do you have an identity that is independent of your parents' influence? Do you still have all the same values, the same religion, the same politics, etc., that your parents had, or do you have some things that are different?" (**I have to answer "yes" to that second part of the question!**)

I learned that as long as one chooses to live in a certain way, it's okay. (Chooses being the keyword here.) However, part of adulthood is discovering what we really believe as a person and how we choose to participate in the world, even if it's a departure from what we learned at home as a child. As an adult, I finally realized I was free to be my authentic self. My parents were also free as they were no longer responsible for me. Everyone got to be themselves! (**It was my newly** discovered "self" that appeared on the beach that day.)

Furthermore, I learned how important it is to discover what we truly believe, even if it's a departure from what we have learned at home. I had discovered during our time in the Air Force that I didn't feel the same way about some things the way my mother did. I'd been subconsciously carrying the rules applied by her to me as a child into my adulthood. **(That's my fault, not her's.)** Why did these inner stirrings start to occur when "we" joined the Air Force? What was the "trigger" that caused me to start expressing my new "self?" Here's what I learned. **It was distance, physical distance.**

The more I've analyzed myself, the more I've come to realize that each time I felt these inner stirrings, I was 200, 500, 1,100, and then 1,600 miles from home. Physical distance was the key to allowing me to be "free." How often have I used that word in these musings? I hope these explanations make it clearer to understand the source of my actions that Saturday. I'll now pick up the story where I left off.

After that Saturday, I felt relieved. Lee J. had seen Alexandra, and he liked what he saw. I liked my Alexandra persona, too. Again, I'll use my oft-repeated phrase. I felt like the bird that had just been let out of its cage, only this time, I had **really** gotten out of the cage.

The last weeks of Lee J.'s training had to be one of the most intense times of his entire life. He had told me earlier that when you add the passion he felt for what he was doing as a pilot, then come home to the passion he felt for me and the kids, he was almost in a sensory overload condition, but he loved it. I was in a similar state myself. Being **far** from home was allowing the Alexandra side of me to emerge, and it was making me a different person in a lot of ways.

As I've previously stated, I loved the attention the kids and I garnered from the increased number of people on the beaches. The summer season was in full swing, and the beach down from our house now had a sizable number of beachgoers every day. It wasn't crowded by any standard, but the vacationers had finally shown up. We had always liked walking that beach. We had done that ever since we'd first moved in and continued to do so. The vacationers were friendly; many would stop, talk, and tell me how cute those little tanned, blond girls were. I was loving it. What woman/mom wouldn't! When Lee J. was with us and saw the attention we garnered, he kept saying he knew for sure that he had "eye candy" beyond compare. He enjoyed it, too.

Before that summer, I'd never been in a situation where I became aware of the kind of attention the girls and I garnered. Lee J. and I had a discussion about all of this. I was curious about what was so special about the kids and me. I truly didn't fully understand it since I'd never experienced it before.

His answer went something like this, "Sandy, you have a hot, beautifully tanned, and toned body, and most of it is exposed due to your 'barely-there' bikini. You've got sun-bleached hair that you keep under control with a hair band that color coordinates with your swimsuit. **Girl, you are put together!** As an added bonus to the scenery you're providing, you've got two of the cutest, best-behaved little blonde-headed girls imaginable in tow, and that, my dear, is the picture people see of the three of y'all."

Furthermore, he said, "The men on the beach see a very beautiful, hot young woman, **but** she's a mom. That takes you 'off the market!' The women on the beach just see a beautiful young mom with two cute little girls. That makes you no threat!"

I think he was probably right in his assessment. The kids and I continued to enjoy being on the beach and meeting many of the vacationers. They seemed to be from everywhere, and the fact we were from Texas could always elicit a conversation. My shyness seemed to disappear during this time. I loved who I was becoming.

The passion Lee J. and I were both experiencing was intense. To say that our pumps were primed for each other would be quite an understatement. The kids were always easy to get to bed, while at the same time, we both needed each other seemingly every night. Though we had been married for almost seven years, our passion levels for each other were now higher than normal, even for us. For me, making love to the guy I loved more than life itself was almost like a spiritual experience. I know that sounds crazy, but that's the way I felt during those final days we were in Florida.

If Lee J. had been on the afternoon flight schedule, and it wasn't too late, he would sometimes go by the O-Club for a "beverage" with some of his new friends. He was never one who stayed very long in those situations, and I wondered just how I should write this section. He suggested using a country song that wasn't even written when all these things were going on with us. This song says what we were feeling far better than anything I could write.

> *Well boys I hate to leave good company*
> *But my baby just called me on the phone*
> *And from the sound of her voice, I simply have no choice*
> *I left something turned on at home*
> *(chorus)*
> *It ain't the stove, it ain't the heater*
> *She's hotter and a whole lot sweeter*
> *All day long she's been there alone*
> *Right now her arms are open, the house is prob'ly smokin'*
> *'Cause I left something turned on at home*
> (*I Left Something Turned on at Home*, Trace Adkins)

We laugh every time we read those lyrics, but we both know that the description fits me perfectly. I was truly **turned on,** waiting for him to come home.

The times we had a full day together were generally on the weekends. After my recent experience on our last picnic, I was ready to go "picnicking" again as soon as we got the chance. We were down to our last two weekends before he would finish his training; we picnicked on both those weekends. For whatever reason, we never saw a soul once we passed the dunes area. I would "go top down" (as Lee J. called it) as soon as we passed the dunes and would stay that way until we were almost back later that afternoon. I'm not sure I was quite as exhilarated as I was during the first picnic outing, but the freedom I felt was always there. It continued to be quite intoxicating.

Not only did we have a couple more topless picnics, but I became intent on having absolutely no tan lines at all by sunbathing topless down in the dunes area two or three times a week, but I never went there unless Lee J. was with us. We would go there if he was on the morning schedule and got home by 1 pm or so. The times we saw anyone, I would just roll over on my stomach until they passed. After three weeks of Saturday picnics and sunbathing topless at the dunes during the week, I had erased any tan lines, and my boobs were as tanned as the rest of my body (excluding what my bikini bottoms covered).

I'm not sure why I wanted everything equally tanned other than it was a way I could prove to both Lee J. and myself I was a different girl than the one I had been when we first got to Florida three months earlier. I certainly was not an entirely new person, but now I had a free spirit side to me. I never let Alexandra emerge at inappropriate times. But Alexandra was always there just below the surface, and I was quite happy to have it that way. I admit that Alexandra also emerged in our bedroom, but I'll have to let you fill in the blanks for that. One other thing, lately, Alexandra's daring sunbathing habits had gotten her boobs very tanned, and Sandy loved getting to wear them that way, too.

July 20 came, and it was over! Lee J. was officially a fully qualified "6" pilot. He had never been more proud of his performance in any of his previous flight training. But now it was time to start paying Uncle Sam back for the money that had been spent to train him to this point. We had been assigned to the 319th FIS at Malmstrom AFB, Great Falls, Montana. It was time to say goodbye to the beach life and say hello to the Big Sky country of Montana.

I should sum up our experiences living on the beach that summer in Florida. I've put a lot of words on these previous pages to cover only four months of our lives. Lee J. and I both think it was a defining time, not only in his Air Force career but in my life, too. During this summer, a long-repressed part of me had the freedom to emerge and become a permanent part of who I was as an authentic person. Though we named this "alter ego" Alexandra, I was still the Sandy he fell in love with and married almost seven years earlier. The Alexandra side of me that I'd found that summer in Florida would become part of my personality, allowing me to become a great salesperson and business owner in the coming years. It helped me to push back my shy and bashful nature and become a person who was just "reserved." I became a young woman that not just anyone could push around. I certainly learned how to be assertive when I needed to be.

Living on the beach had allowed me to embrace the free spirit I'd been secretly longing to have. Being over a thousand miles from home had been the trigger for letting me dress like I wanted to, to be the mom I wanted to be for our kids, and to be the wife and lover I wanted to be for Lee J. I don't know if all of this could have ever happened anywhere else if it hadn't been for our four months in Florida in 1971. We both look back on it as **the** most unforgettable summer of our lives. We are both blessed even today because of that summer.

I'll close with one additional detail. Just prior to leaving Florida, I quit taking my birth control pills, "We needed another baby!"

ROCKY MOUNTAIN HIGH

On April 6, 1972, I was still three weeks from my due date, but I had been sick with a stomach bug, and late that afternoon, I just didn't feel right. I told Lee J. to better get me checked at the hospital. Several friends from the squadron had volunteered to keep the kids when the time came, then not one of them could be found. So, the only alternative was to drop the kids off at the base nursery. **They were not happy!** It was around 7:30 pm when we got to the hospital. Sure enough, I was in labor. Again, this was before dads were allowed in the delivery room. Lee J. was sent to wait in the expectant dad's waiting room.

As usual, it wasn't going to take long. The only excitement was when the nurse went to update Lee J. and told him that she was pretty good at ascertaining the sex of the baby by listening to its heartbeat. She predicted it was a boy. He was not prepared for that because he just assumed that, again, he couldn't "put the stem on the apple," so to speak. So, he grabbed one of the books with boys' names in it that was on the table. He began looking through it for some ideas for this unexpected boy child.

A short time later, the same nurse came in and told him she had been wrong; it was a girl. He says he was disappointed for about five minutes and then was perfectly fine with being the dad of another girl. I'm sure that I was meant to be the mom of girls, therefore, he got to be the dad of girls. Looking back, he will tell you, he wouldn't have had it any other way. He had inherited Raymond's love of little girls. Later, maybe he didn't feel that way quite so much when those little girls became teenagers. I think he spent those years in a state of bewilderment. Let me just say, "He was baffled!"

He came in to see me a short time later and asked me what I wanted him to do about the kids. I told him I would be fine and he should take them home. I would see him in the morning—that's what he did.

The next morning brought bad news. The doctor came in right after Lee J. got there and told us that Marnie Jae—the name was chosen sometime earlier—was very sick and the next 24 hours would be critical. It seemed that she had aspirated during the delivery, and they would require 24 hours to identify what was causing her pneumonia. The pediatrician had put her on a broad-spectrum antibiotic, hoping to have made the right call. Lee J. had seen Marnie just before coming to the room, and he later told me she was a deep color of blue. We were scared!

Those were the days before neonatal intensive care units (NICU) were available at most hospitals, but Marnie's pediatrician had basically set her up in her own private NICU unit at the Malmstrom AFB hospital. She had a pediatric nurse with her around the clock during this time, and she was constantly on the monitors. I prayed; Lee J. prayed; we prayed together that our little girl would be okay. The next morning, she was much improved, and we got to see her. She was so little compared to the size of her sisters when they were born. Her color was still not great, but she was improving. The doctor had guessed right about the proper antibiotic. She was going to be okay.

One of the people we made friends with while living in the apartment when we first got to Great Falls was Dr. Ed Goldberg. He told us sometime later that Marnie could not have been in a better hospital for her condition anywhere. He said the doctor who was her pediatrician was unbelievably talented. He had opted to let the Air Force pay for his medical school in return for a three-year commitment to the Air Force. He was at Malmstrom at this time, fulfilling that commitment. He had recently finished his residency at the Mayo Clinic under a world-renowned pediatrician, and our baby was the beneficiary of his substantial skills. I don't generally say things like this, but Lee J. and I both believe that his being there at the right time for our baby was a "God thing." I'm so sorry that I don't remember his name, but I thank him to this day.

Mother flew up to Great Falls a couple of days later to help me. It was the strangest thing to come home from the hospital without a baby to hold. We went to see her at least once a day, and after a few days, we got to hold her. She was so little! She was precious! Hence, her name, "Sweet Baby Precious" that she carries even today. After twelve long days, we got to bring her home. **Her sisters loved her immediately.**

We had been blessed again with a beautiful little girl. Though her arrival had been far different than the arrival of her two older sisters, she immediately became a part of our family—we were now complete.

How had we made the transition from the beaches of Florida to the majesty that was Montana? We had now added a new member to the Everitt clan. Well, let me catch you up.

Lee J. flew his last flight in Florida on July 16th and didn't have to report at Malmstrom AFB until August 6th. It took a few days to get everything ready to leave Mexico Beach, and we were in no particular hurry. We made time for our last "special picnic" and to bid goodbye to the friends we had made. What a summer we had experienced!

It had been two years when Lee J. had laid out what he thought he could do if "we" joined the Air Force. I don't think, as we left Florida, he could quite believe he had more than achieved his goal. The man I so adored had done it. He will say, "We had done it," and I guess we had. I was so proud of him, and I know he was proud of me and our girls. He especially seemed to like who I was becoming, as did I. Alexandra was definitely going to make the trip to Montana with us. I no longer had all the perplexing feelings just below the surface that I'd had earlier in our Florida stay. Alexandra was becoming a part of who I was. I suppose she was still somewhat below the surface, but she was there nonetheless. I was comfortable with myself.

We took our time getting to Montana by way of Idalou. It was to be a long trip of almost 2,500 miles. The kids were only five and three, and there was a lot of driving to do. So, we stopped many times along the way for breaks and sightseeing.

It took us the better part of 3 days to get to Lubbock. We spent about a week there and got to see and visit with everyone.

I should mention that we figured out after Marnie was born that she was conceived at my parent's house. There was not a lot of privacy there, but I guess it was private enough for Lee J. to get me pregnant. As I revealed in the last chapter, I'd quit taking my birth control pills just before we left Florida. It sure hadn't taken long for me to get pregnant. Lee J. used to laugh and say he was definitely married to "Fertile Myrtle." I guess he was.

The ones who had come to Florida to see us were still talking about how much they had enjoyed their stay. There were some comments made about how tan we all were. Little did they know how totally tanned one of us was. Lee J. kidded me about keeping the secret that I had no tan lines where my bikini top was supposed to have been. I curtly told him to keep his mouth shut. I said Alexandra really didn't care if people knew, but if Sandy wanted people to know how tan her boobs were, she would do the telling. He complied and kept his mouth shut. I'm not sure if anybody ever really knew how much time I'd spent "topless" during our Mexico Beach adventures. Alexandra was definitely going with us to Montana, but I wasn't sure that Sandy was ready to disclose that little tidbit of information to my mother just yet.

I guess I'd inherited my mother's love of traveling because I began to anticipate the drive to Montana. It would be through a part of the country neither Lee J. nor I had ever seen.

The distance was close to 1,500 miles from Idalou, and of course, my daddy was worried about his kiddos making such a long trek. To start our trip, we planned a stop in Amarillo to see Tootie and Ann. Raymond and Gwen drove up with us. It was nice to have us all together because we knew it would be a while before we would have the chance again.

It was to be a long drive, and we planned on seeing the sights as much as possible along the way. The new car we had bought in Sherman had an "ultra-modern eight-track cassette player," so we bought some new tapes for the trip. I don't remember what we had, but the Carpenters' tape and Glen Campbell's latest were among them. Even today, when we hear *Close to You* or *By the Time I Get to Phoenix*, Lee J. and I both look at each other and say, "The Montana trip." It's funny how something like a song can trigger memories of days long gone by, but those songs will be forever tied to that drive to Montana in 1971.

I don't remember what I had for the kids to keep them busy while we drove, but I don't remember them being much trouble at all. They had all their books, dolls, and stuff in the back seat—that car was loaded. Lee J. had that trunk packed in every nook and cranny possible, and we laughed when we saw how low the rear end was setting.

We went up into Colorado and to the Royal Gorge. I do not like heights and being on that bridge was not fun for me. I'm glad we saw it, but it sure ramped up my anxiety. After leaving, I thought the drive through Colorado was fantastic. If I had ever been to Colorado before on a family vacation, it was when I was little and could not appreciate it. We didn't make the drive up Pikes Peak on this trip. If Lee J. had any thoughts of driving up there, he quickly dropped them after seeing how nervous the Royal Gorge had made me.

We saw several of the sights in Colorado, and I especially enjoyed the beauty of Seven Falls. From Colorado, it was on to Wyoming, which was certainly uncharted territory for us. The Grand Tetons National Park and the mountains there were more than beautiful. They were just awesome. When I said earlier that I was anticipating the drive to Montana, little did I know just how much I would enjoy this experience. My mother's love of traveling was certainly coming out in me.

We continued our drive after leaving Wyoming and crossed into Montana. We came upon this place where they had a stocked trout pond, but only the kids could fish. Of course, they had helpers to help the kids catch the trout. Part of the deal was they would cook what the kids caught as part of a meal for the whole family. This turned out to be a bit expensive but also quite a hoot for our girls.

We rolled into Great Falls, Montana, on Friday, August 4th. Lee J. had to sign in on base by Sunday, so for the rest of Friday and Saturday, we had some time to kill. The weather was definitely not what I had expected. It was almost 100 degrees and was expected to be the same the next day. They told us that this was not the norm. It did cause me a little stir because motels that far north were not all air-conditioned in those days. There was no way I planned to stay in a hot motel room. We had to go to two or three different motels before we found an air-conditioned one. As soon as we checked in, I gave the kids shorts to wear and put on shorts and a halter myself. In fact, I got out one of the sets that I'd made in Florida, where we all matched. We now had an air-conditioned place to stay, and we girls had something cool to wear. Lee J. laughed and said it sure changed everybody's attitude completely. Yes, it did!

We left the motel and set out to explore the town. One of the first things we saw was that the Montana State Fair was in town, and Glen Campbell was to be in concert that night at the fairgrounds. After listening to one of his tapes countless times on the way to Montana, who would have thought we would have the opportunity to hear him live the first night we were in Great Falls? We got our tickets and made plans to go hear Glen that night. It was still really hot, and we still had on our outfits from earlier in the day. As we were entering the fairgrounds and heading for the grandstands, I turned and softly told Lee J. that I thought a lot of people were staring at us. Lee J.'s "eye candy" that night must have been quite a sight for the locals. I was a young mom in shorts and a halter who had two little tanned blondies with me. In our beach outfits, we obviously stood out from the rest of the crowd, especially since it all matched. *Seems Alexandra and her kids could turn heads in Montana, too.* I loved it!

The concert was great, but we were tired; it had been a long journey. Though I was still pumped at how much fun I was having, I guess I was still in vacation mode. Saturday, we started looking around to see what kind of rental property was available. Lee J. said we should try to get base housing if we could. However, he had talked to someone while we were in Florida who was familiar with Malmstrom AFB, and they had informed him that base housing for a first lieutenant was probably not going to happen. That was exactly the way it turned out to be when he started the sign-in process at the base. We would have to live off base, and that was fine with me.

We decided to look for an unfurnished apartment. We just didn't have a good feeling for what we needed. The decision on the apartment turned out to be the right one for the time being. We moved in and got somewhat settled within a week.

Lee J. had a lot of new guy stuff to get through, and he got busy very quickly. He loved it. The camaraderie of a fighter squadron was something he truly relished, and he was loving flying. He was finally paying the Air Force back for all they had invested in his training. It was around September 1st when he was assigned his first alert shift. That meant he would not be at home at all for the 24 hours he was on alert. I realized this was going to be a part of our new life that I didn't much care for.

Before I talk about starting school for Julie in Montana, I should first explain how she had learned so much at a very young age. During the three weeks Lee J. was in Air Force Survival School the year before, I had stayed with Mother and Daddy. Julie went to Barb and Mama Gracie's kindergarten in Idalou in that period. She learned all her phonics during that short time and began to teach herself to read. I bought her all kinds of workbooks, puzzles, and such to help her along. She thought it was fun. She could literally read most of a newspaper to me. She certainly did not comprehend all she was reading, but she could sound the words out. She was one smart kid. So, this was the little person who was starting kindergarten in Great Falls.

School started around September 01st, and I got Julie signed up to start kindergarten. I went with her that first Monday and met her teacher. I explained to her that Julie could already read almost anything and that if they wanted to move her up, that would be fine with me. I already knew that there wasn't much they were going to teach in kindergarten that she didn't already know. The teacher was nice enough, but she was pretty condescending to Julie's mom, Alexandra. She explained that there was so much more than just reading in what they were going to teach her. Alexandra could tell she should just back off and let the chips fall where they may.

The next Thursday, I/Alexandra got a call from the teacher; she wanted a parent-teacher conference. I told Lee J. about the call when he came home that evening, and he was like, "How can a little kid like Julie get into trouble in the first week of school?" He said it took him a lot longer than that. I think he was trying to be funny. He was! I was concerned though, but there was no need to have been concerned at all.

The teacher told me that in all her years of teaching, she'd had only one other student like Julie, and they had moved that little girl up. She also said that Julie was ahead of where the previously mentioned little girl had been and that Julie's maturity was unbelievable. She indicated she had used Julie as kind of a teacher's aid the previous day or so. Lee J. tells everyone that Julie was kicked out of kindergarten after only four days. He says it's a record. Seriously, she was moved to the 1st grade and immediately was put in their GT program. The girl's got some genes!

As I stated previously, I'd quit taking my birth control pills just before we left Florida. I knew I was pregnant for a good while before I went to the doctor at the base hospital. They calculated my due date to be in late April.

So now, we've got a new baby coming, Lee J. has settled into a routine at the squadron, and we started thinking about buying a house. The apartment we were living in was not going to easily accommodate us with a baby. At the time, we figured we would be in Montana for three years. That was the normal term for a first assignment, so we started looking for a house to buy. We found a three-bedroom house with a full basement that was partially finished, which was in our price range. We bought it and moved in around November 01st.

Now that we had a house, we decided we needed a dog. Lee J. had seen a lot of Labradors around town but really didn't know anything about them. He talked to some of the guys in the squadron, and everybody said, "Labs could not be beat if you wanted a hunting dog and a family dog all in one package."

We started looking for some Lab pups for sale. There was an ad in the newspaper that caught our attention, so we went over to look at the litter. There were seven or eight yellow pups in the litter, and they were about a week away from weaning. The girls picked out a little female that they were sure was made just for them. The fact that they weren't ready to wean gave Lee J. time to get a place ready to keep a puppy. She was going to be an outside dog, so she needed a good doghouse that could be heated. He also built a small run so we could keep her confined outside, although the kids would keep her inside with them a lot.

We went for our new family member the next week. We named her Fancy, and did the kids ever love her! We had our house; we had our dog; Julie was doing great in school; Lee J. loved everything about his job. More than once, he told me that he couldn't believe he was getting paid to do the things he was getting to do. I was excited about having another baby. The only downside was I really didn't like having to be by myself when he was on alert. Frankly, being pregnant and hardly knowing any of our neighbors was more than a little disconcerting at times. But all in all, it was good. Alexandra was coping!

As winter started to set in, I realized that Montana was going to be a lot different than Texas. We soon got our first snow. I always thought when it snowed this far north it stayed until spring. Not so in Montana; there was a thing called Chinook winds that could warm things up for a few days. The snow would be gone until the next snow which could be two days or two weeks later when the weather got bad again.

As Christmas approached, we found out there were places we could go and cut our own Christmas tree. The kids and the dog were all in for another adventure, so we all loaded into the car and literally headed for the hills. We found just the right tree, Lee J. cut it down, and then we hauled it back to the house. Such fun! There were so many things we got to do that I'd never dreamed of. This was one of them. What a change all of this was from the summer we had just spent on the beach in Florida. I was really enjoying what we were doing. Again, the only downside was the nights Lee J. had to pull "alert." My anxiety issues would ramp up, but again, Alexandra was learning to cope.

After Christmas, I suspect Raymond called my mother and asked his famous question, "Evelyn, don't you think it's time we got those kids home for a visit?"

They called and asked if we could come for a visit if we had some help with the airfare. We said yes, and we flew home in late January for about a week. It was great because I did miss everybody at home from time to time. The other thing was that it was considerably warmer in Idalou than it was in Montana during January. We had a great visit, but soon, we made the flight back to Great Falls.

I was very pregnant by this time, and I didn't think I would be making any more long trips until after the baby was born. So, we didn't, but that didn't stop us from utilizing the pickup camper we had bought for some close-to-home excursions with the girls and Fancy. We had bought a pickup and camper that became Lee J.'s pride and joy. He had a "boot" made to allow access to the camper from the cab of the pickup. That way, the kids and the dog could ride in the back. We would have great fun in that rig the rest of the time we were in the Air Force. The girls absolutely loved going camping, and so did the dog.

Sometime after our return from Idalou in January, I had the worst experience of my life concerning one of the kids. My daily routine was to stay at home during the day with Angie while Julie was at school. It was getting close to time to either walk or drive (depending on the weather) the two blocks to Julie's school. I called Angie, and she didn't come running or answer. I started looking for her, then started yelling for her, and there was no answer. I started to panic. I looked everywhere and still couldn't find her. I even tried going to the neighbors who were either unfriendly or unconcerned. I finally went back into the house to look once more, and this time, I happened to glance behind the couch. Lo and behold, there she was, sound asleep between the couch and the wall. I didn't know whether to hug her or spank her. I hugged her; I cried. I had never been that terrified before. Somehow, I got myself together, and we went to get Julie. I have never forgotten the awful feeling of thinking that my child is gone and not knowing where she is.

Losing Angie that day was traumatic, and it took me a while to get over it. For the first time ever, I experienced a real terror. Losing a child and not knowing her whereabouts was devastating for me. I've never forgotten the awful feeling I had that day.

I started this chapter with the situation we had with Marnie's birth. Her addition to our family was obviously the high point of our time in Montana. But the fact that the happy ending we had could have just as easily gone the other way really affected me. I had been lulled into a sense of complacency since both my earlier pregnancies had been without any serious drama. The fact that Mother had flown to Montana and had been there for me during the long twelve-day wait to bring Marnie home from the hospital had helped a lot. Though she was there for only two days after we brought Marnie home, her presence during the wait had been a great boost to my morale. I told her more than once how much I appreciated her being there for me. She would just smile when I said that. Though I had not always agreed with her about some things, she was there when I needed her. I knew she loved me, and I loved her. I've tried to model her love for me with my own kids.

About the time Mama Gracie had to leave, Raymond and Gwen also flew up to help us out. I loved Raymond's interaction with Julie and Angie. That man did love his granddaughters, and they loved him back. Gwen was a big help also, and I trusted her completely. The fact she was an RN certainly helped in that regard. I was able to get some much-needed rest. Marnie was so much smaller than the other two had been, but she came home to us completely healthy. That baby got plenty of attention from all of us.

As we settled in as a family of five, the rumors we'd been hearing turned out to be true. The Air Force was realigning its air defense forces, and we were to be reassigned to Grand Forks AFB in North Dakota that June. We really hated to leave Montana, but orders were orders. We decided to make the most of our time left and planned a trip down to Yellowstone when Marnie was about six weeks old. Today, I think, "What was I thinking?" The answer is, we were young and thought nothing about it. We loaded up the camper with a six-year-old, a four-year-old, a six-week-old, a big yellow dog, and a young couple who were having the time of their lives.

The trip to Yellowstone would be the last of the Montana excursions before we left for North Dakota. It was towards the end of May when we made that trip. We were gone for three days. The drive was about four hours in a camper with our crew, and we spent about a day and a half in the park. As usual, the kids had a blast, but a six-week-old baby was a different story. I noticed, looking at the pictures before I wrote this, that I appeared tired, and I'm sure I was. Yet, I enjoyed the trip immensely and have vivid memories of it even today, over fifty years later.

We returned from the three-day trip to Yellowstone and began to put preparations together for the move to Grand Forks AFB. Our time in Montana would only total about ten months instead of the three years that we initially expected, but it was an event-packed ten months.

Most of the time we were there, I was pregnant with Marnie, but I didn't let the pregnancy keep me from doing a lot of things. I haven't mentioned several things that we squeezed into the time we lived there. Lee J. and the girls went ice skating on one of the ponds in a city park not far from the house two or three times during the winter. I opted out of trying ice skating. I knew I had weak ankles and falling was not one of the things a pregnant woman wants to have happen. We made the drive down to Helena one weekend to see the capital, plus we made a trip over to Glacier National Park on another occasion. Looking back, we were busy.

The one thing I never got used to during our time in Montana was being by myself with the kids a lot when Lee J. was on alert. Though he was close by in case of an emergency, he was not available for much of what I needed at times. It forced me to become much more capable than ever before just to run our household without much help. I got really good at it, but I did not like it. This would change drastically for the better when we got to live on base at Grand Forks.

I know I have referred to myself as Alexandra several times during this chapter. Those last weeks in Florida had a lasting effect on some of the subconscious feelings I was able to release during that last month there. I think, during our ten months in Montana my personality was becoming a mix of both Sandy and Alexandra. The fact that I was still far from home was allowing the process that started in Florida to continue while we were stationed in Montana.

Montana turned out to be a time with a lot of drama. Marnie's birth was far from what I had experienced in my two previous pregnancies; I spent some uncomfortable nights alone with just the kids while Lee J. was on alert; I really didn't develop any close friendships during this time; the trauma of "losing" Angie, albeit for a brief time. All that taken together was a lot to process. But I got through it, and I think the strength of my newly discovered Alexandra persona helped me to cope with everything without withdrawing, as my Sandy persona wanted to do in days gone by. The process would continue.

Lee J.'s orders show us leaving Montana on June 10, 1972, with a report date of June 30. We would have 20 days to move, so we planned a detour to Idalou on our way to North Dakota. We had two vehicles to move to our new station, and Lee J. asked the squadron scheduler if he drove our car 750 miles to Grand Forks; could he catch a ride back to Montana in one of the squadron's F-106B models (a two-seater) and call it a training sortie? The DO (Director of Operations) at the squadron approved it, and a few days before we were to depart, he drove our car to Grand Forks and spent the night in the VOQ. He had taken his flight gear with him, and one of his buddies picked him up the next day in the B model and brought him back to Malmstrom. It took over 12 hours to drive the distance and a little over an hour to fly back. The "Six" was one fast airplane!

Our trip to Texas in the camper was long but uneventful. I'll pick up the trip from Idalou to North Dakota in the next chapter. It was also long but quite eventful.

Grand Time in Grand Forks

It was June of 1972, and the Everitt clan was in the process of a PCS (Permanent Change of Station) move to Lee J.'s new assignment to Grand Forks AFB, N.D. It was to be the same job he had done in Montana, only about 750 miles east in North Dakota. We drove from Montana to Idalou in three days in our pickup camper. I don't remember exactly how long we stayed for the visit, but long enough for me to be ready to get on with our move. We would take three days to cover almost 1,300 miles. With a 6-year-old, a 4-year-old, and a 2-month-old plus our dog Fancy, Lee J. wanted to make it enjoyable. We could spend one night in the camper and one in a motel. Once we got north of Oklahoma, the country would be all new to us, so taking our time made sense.

We left Idalou after lunch with the idea of spending the night somewhere in Oklahoma when everybody got tired. The first problem was that the pickup Lee J. had bought in Montana was not air-conditioned. It was never a problem up north, but it became a problem for us that day. It was a hot Texas day in June, and holding a two-month-old was not a way to stay cool. To top off the heat problem, we were in Oklahoma City around ten o'clock that night when the left rear tire blew out as we were on an overpass on the main north-south freeway. There was not much of a shoulder to pull over on, and the passing traffic was too close for comfort for us in the camper. Lee J. started to change the tire and realized that the jack he had would not raise the pickup with the camper on it. I was more than a little nervous. He was, too.

He'd seen a filling station about a quarter mile back and decided to walk back and see if he could borrow a jack. He started walking back down the overpass, making me scared. Every time a truck blew past us, the camper swayed. Meanwhile, he borrowed a floor jack from the filling station and dragged that thing up the hill to the pickup. He got the tire changed; all the while, he was way too close to the passing traffic. He got through and decided that rather than trying to find his way back to the filling station from that spot on the freeway, he would just drag the jack back. So off he went, and we had to wait for a few minutes until he got back. By now, though, the temperature had cooled off some and the heat became less of a problem. I was relieved but mentally exhausted.

In fact, we were both exhausted, both mentally and physically. The kids were tired, too. The map showed a rest stop not far north of Oklahoma City, so we headed for it. When we got there and I got everyone settled in, we spent the night in the camper at the rest stop. We had plenty of provisions, and the rest stop had bathrooms, so we were okay.

The next morning, we made our way to the next town of any size and bought a new spare tire and a good jack that would lift the pickup with the camper on it. We got ourselves settled in and headed north. Later in the day, either Julie or Angie started getting sick and running a fever. (I don't remember which one it was.) However, we were nearing Omaha, Nebraska, where Offutt AFB was located. We headed for the base ER to get our sick one looked at. We spent some time there, and they gave us some medicine that seemed to help with the problem. We decided to look for a place to spend the night in a motel. I don't remember where we stopped, but it was in the Omaha area. This trip had become more of an adventure than I had signed up for. Lee J. was a bit frazzled himself, but he kept his cool and found us a nice motel. We finally settled in for the night and got some much-needed rest.

We left the next morning from the motel with our sights set on getting to Grand Forks that day, and we did. We got a motel room in town before going to the base the next day to sign in and get our car. I was so glad to have my car back, and Lee J. was too. We both had had enough of the camper for a while.

Upon signing in, Lee J. learned it was standard practice for those in the squadron who were on an accompanied TDY assignment to make their house available to incoming squadron members while they waited for a house on base to become available. We were to stay in Captain Boddy's house until we got base housing assigned. Captain Boddy was TDY to SOS (Squadron Officer School) and would be gone for a couple more months. Everything in the house was available for our use. What a deal, but it made me nervous because the

Boddy's didn't have children, and we did.

We moved what we had into their house. I made sure the girls understood that they had to be careful, and they were. Lee J. was still going through all the in-processing when he got a call from the command center to report to the housing office. **We had a house assigned.** What we were afraid would stretch out several weeks turned out to be three days. Two days later our household goods arrived; we now had a home. It was too good to be true, but it was true. We left the Boddy's house just as we had found it, but I was so thankful for getting to stay there.

Our new home was a two-story, four-bedroom duplex at Grand Forks AFB. It was spacious, and **it was on the base.** I felt safe for the 20 months we lived there. Lee J. could pull a 15-minute alert from home if it was on the weekend. He would go in and sleep at the alert barn, but for me it was a far better situation than what I had dealt with in Great Falls.

I soon met the person who would become my best friend during our time in North Dakota. Marilyn Moore lived on the same side of the duplex located next door to the south, which meant there was a family living on the other side of their duplex between us. However, we always considered them our next-door neighbors anyway. I don't recall the circumstances of how we met, but most likely, she brought something over to welcome us to the neighborhood. We immediately bonded. She had three girls, very nearly the same age as mine. Hers were Mary, Angie, and Laura. We **both** had a middle child named Angie. Soon, we were meeting for morning coffee, keeping the other's kids while the other ran an errand. All the normal things that stay-at-home moms do for each other and their kids. I'd never had that before, and I quickly learned to love it.

We were as different as daylight and dark. Initially, I must have put on my Sandy demeanor while Marilyn entered the room mouth first. I soon learned what an "outgoing" person she was. She loved her kids dearly, but she was not the hovering mom that I was. She was always smiling, with a giggle not far behind. She was a lot like I wanted my Alexandra persona to be; maybe that's why I immediately liked her so much. David, her husband, was a KC135 pilot, and he wasn't nearly as outgoing as Marilyn was. They say opposites attract, and those two certainly did. Lee J. and Dave had a lot in common since they were both Air Force pilots, but the flying they did was far different. However, they could still talk about flying.

Marilyn and Alexandra soon started lying out together like I used to lay out with my sisters before getting married. There's just something about enjoying the outdoors with a good friend. We could watch the kids together and talk. I'd not had that since becoming an adult. It just made my life that much better. The previous summer, we had been in Florida, and now, once more, I was enjoying getting a tan. Being around her was letting the freedom I'd felt the year before start to take hold of me again. Alexandra had made it to North Dakota.

By late August, we learned Mother and Daddy were

planning a trip up to see us. It was starting to feel like Florida all over again because Raymond and Gwen were planning to come in October. I was loving it. Living on base was perfect for me; I always felt safe. Lee J. was ecstatic about his job. He loved the new CO (Commanding Officer) and was beginning to fly some advanced tactical training that he said was making him a real fighter pilot. I had no idea what he was talking about. He seemed like a real fighter pilot to me already. He swaggered around like one anyway.

Mother and Daddy flew up in late August for a week, and one of our excursions was up to Winnipeg, Canada. Winnipeg was about a 2 1/2-hour drive from Grand Forks; this was the first of several trips we made up there during our time in North Dakota. Winnipeg was a beautiful place, and Mother loved it. She loved to travel far more than Daddy, but he would endure a flight to get to see his kids. I do think he really enjoyed his excursion into Canada, though. We also went over to Minnesota while they were with us. When they say Minnesota is the land of a thousand lakes, they mean it. It was beautiful over there. They stayed about a week and the kids loved the attention from Ma-ma and Pa-pa while they were here. But like every visit from kinfolks from West Texas, too soon, they were gone.

I talk about being in Grand Forks, but that is a bit misleading. There's Grand Forks, North Dakota, and then there's Grand Forks AFB, North Dakota. They are not co-located. The base is 14 miles west of the city, just north of the town of Emerado. We lived on base, but of course, we traveled into town regularly. The BX (Base Exchange) and the commissary had most of what we needed, so it was convenient to stay supplied without going into town. In the winter, going into town could be an ordeal. There were days when the weather never got above zero. It was too much trouble to get the kids out in weather like that, so we didn't; I never went by myself if Lee J. wasn't available.

Julie went to school in the fall after we got there; it was close enough that she could walk even in the coldest of weather. I would stand on the front porch and watch her all the way to the school door about a block away. Lee J. kids me about wearing shorts all winter, and I did. However, I did not stand out on the porch in shorts to make sure Julie got to school if it was terribly cold. I had to bundle up pretty well to be out even for five minutes. It was so convenient not to have to get the other two out and in the car to take Julie to school. The coldest weather happened in December, January, and February, so it wasn't an all-year thing. The winter weather was harsh, but we enjoyed our time there. Lee J. loved his job, Alexandra had a best friend next door, and we had a great social life with all the squadron parties and activities.

I haven't mentioned Fancy since I started this chapter. She was about nine months old when we left Montana. Lee J. really loved training her, and she was so easy to train. There was an old rock quarry just north of the base with perfectly clear water and a little sandy beach the kids could play on while he worked with his dog. He had a retrieving dummy launcher he used at the quarry. It would launch a dummy 75 yards either into the water or over it on the other bank. Fancy loved the water and loved retrieving those dummies. It was fun to watch. She had an outside kennel but spent a lot of time with the kids in the house. Lee J. found some places to take her to hunt. He certainly enjoyed that dog, and the girls and I did, too.

I'd never been more content since we'd joined the Air Force. My family was complete, and our living situation was great. Lee J. loved me, the kids, the dog, and his job. I continued to enjoy the time Marilyn and I spent together. As I said earlier, we had truly become best friends. We generally would see each other every day. She was so outgoing and friendly.

I'm sure that Marilyn was the reason that the process I described earlier continued during our time in North Dakota. Lee J. would tell me Marilyn was giving Alexandra some OJT (on-the-job training). She was so entertaining. When we were at their house or vice-versa, we tended to get a bit silly. After we got to know each other better, she would become somewhat unfiltered. I was learning to be the same way. I could be hilarious. Lee J. would just roll his eyes and grin, and I took that as his approval of this part of his wife. I liked who I was becoming.

In October, Raymond, Gwen, and Neil Faulkner visited us. Gwen had told Lee J. that Neil was coming with them. We both thought that this sounded a bit strange, but Neil was fun to be around, so we didn't give it a lot of thought. We just didn't know the whole story.

Neil was the same age as Lee J., which made Raymond and Neil a full generation apart in age, but they had become very close friends. He knew that Raymond's health was different from what we had been led to believe. The facts were that his friend, Raymond, was a lot sicker than we knew. Neil worried that they were not up to the trip to Grand Forks by themselves, so he offered to come with them. They accepted his offer. The truth was he brought them to North Dakota rather than just tagging along with them. Once we knew the whole story a year or so later, our appreciation of what he did was considerable.

After they arrived, we showed them around the area and asked what they wanted to do. They weren't particular, so we suggested to start with a trip to Winnipeg. Of course, we had been there a couple of months earlier when my folks had visited, so we knew a little about where to go. They had come to see us and the kids; all the sights we saw were secondary. We made our excursion to Winnipeg, and I think Raymond decided that traveling and going to restaurants could be a bit daunting with six-month-old Marnie. Let's just say she was not fond of eating out and neither was I after a couple of stops to get something to eat. She was just six months old; what can I say?

Once we got back home, she became the happy Marnie I knew. How Raymond loved little girls! I've said before that Lee J. got his love for little girls from his dad. Too bad Raymond didn't live long enough to enjoy them as they grew. He would have been one proud Pa-pa!

The three of them stayed about a week and it turned out to be so special for us. But as always, too soon, the visit was over, and life returned to normal. Little did we know that Raymond had only about a year to live. I guess it's because of that I still cherish the memory of their visit even today, fifty years later. Lee J. and I thanked Neil later for making that trip possible for Raymond and Gwen.

We made plans for Lee J. to take leave and drive home in early January 1973. After talking with Jon Davis, his T-37 instructor at Sheppard, we decided to stop at Wichita Falls on the way and spend one night with Jon and Mary. Jon had been the buyer of the infamous $1 blue pickup Lee J. drove during pilot training. He and Jon had remained in touch ever since we left Sheppard. They cooked up a duck hunting trip for early the next morning after we spent the night with them. We had already made plans to bring Fancy with us, so the guys going duck hunting was part of the plan. Little did we know the tragedy in store for our dog on that hunt.

They were hunting by a lake close to Wichita Falls. Fancy got an inch cut on her right shoulder as they crossed an old, barbed wire fence on the edge of the lake. Lee J. didn't even notice it until they started to go back to the pickup. He thought it didn't look like much at all. When they got back to Jon's house mid-morning, we cleaned it a bit, then loaded up the kids and Fancy and headed to Idalou. Fancy had been fantastic that morning while they shot the ducks. Jon was really impressed with how good she was, especially since she was just a little over a year old. He had grown up in Alabama and had been around retrievers all his life, yet he was impressed. Lee J. was so proud of her. As usual, she rode cuddled up between Julie and Angie in the back seat. She was just another sister to those kids.

We got to Raymond and Gwen's house late that afternoon, and the plan was to spend the night with them. Gwen made Fancy a bed in the kitchen. The next morning, we were shocked to see Fancy's shoulder. It was swollen three or four times its regular size, and she was in obvious pain. Gwen said it looked like a bad infection. Raymond called the vet he used; it was a Saturday, and the vet had planned to be off that day, but he agreed to meet them at his office as soon as they could get there.

When they arrived and took Fancy in, the doc took one look and said it looked like a virulent strain of staph to him. He said these were almost impossible to clear up. He drained it and examined her further and then told Lee J. that he wasn't sure he could save Fancy. The only hope she had was to amputate the leg at the shoulder, but he made no guarantees. Lee J. was devastated. He made the choice to put her down. He told me later that it was almost impossible to wrap his head around the fact that 24 hours earlier, he was duck hunting with Fancy, and now he had to walk out of the vet's office with just her collar. I'd never seen my guy so sad!

He'd had dogs before, but never had he had one that he had become so close to. There's no telling how many hours he'd spent training her during her time with our family. She had been the most eager of pupils who always wanted to please. I have such fond memories of her in the water at the rock quarry. She seemed to never get tired and always wanted more. The girls loved to go places with her curled up between them in the back seat of the car or riding in the back of the camper with them when we went out in it. She was an integral part of our family. We all missed her, but like I said, I'd never seen my husband so sad. He was definitely going through a grieving process. On the drive home from Texas, we talked about what we wanted to do. We decided to start looking for another Lab puppy as soon as we got back to Grand Forks, and that's what we did.

After returning home, we started looking for another Lab. This time, we found some folks in Thief River Falls, Minnesota, who were selling some black Labradors. We took the kids over for the selection and the only stipulation was that the pup be female. They had picked out Fancy, and we were sure they could pick out another one just as good as Fancy had been. We were both still grieving a bit over losing her, but another pup was just the answer for me, and I think Lee J., too. We came home with a black Lab we named Pixie. She would be with us for many years to come. Lee J. decided he also would like to train a pointing type of dog shortly after we got Pixie. It would be March before he found just the setter he wanted from a breeder down in Oklahoma. The breeder air-freighted her to us, and we all went to the airport to meet our newest family member. The kids and I loved her immediately. She was as sweet as honey, hence her name. I liked Lee J.'s interest in training these dogs because most of it was done in the huge back area between our base housing and the perimeter fence. He could work with the dogs there, even if he was on a 15-minute alert. What a deal!

Julie and Angie were having the time of their lives with their little sister and the dogs. To them, Marnie was a bit like a living doll. It was idyllic. Upon reflection, I think I found myself the most content I had ever known up to that point in my life. I was 26 years old and had three beautiful girls, ages seven, five, and one. I had a loving husband who was having the time of his life flying USAF F-106s for a living. Though he was busy with work, he did a good job showing how much he loved me and his girls (that included his 2 girl dogs) by being with us whenever he was off. Our relationship had never been better in every aspect. It's crazy how high our passion had remained. He used to laugh and say that the one thing he had learned being married to me was the foreplay I liked best involved him taking out the trash or loading the dishwasher. He was right. The only downside to this time in our lives was his alert duty. But since we lived on base, he could be at home on weekends if he was on 15-minute alert duty. He had to sleep in the alert barn, so sleeping together was not possible about once or maybe twice a week. I always missed sleeping together.

It's been more than 50 years, as I write this, yet I don't remember us having much conflict at all. There really wasn't much to argue about. Lee J. was paid enough for us to live comfortably. He spent most of his off time with us, and we girls, especially me, loved him dearly. After the arrival of

Honey, Lee J. had two dogs to work with. He would generally work with them every day as the weather warmed up. I used to watch him out the kitchen window as he worked with Pixie on her retrieving and Honey on her pointing. I wouldn't exactly call what he was doing "work." He looked like a guy playing with his dogs.

My friendship with Marilyn continued to thrive as we spent some time together almost every day. With warmer weather coming on, we had started lying out together again. I was enjoying getting some time in the sun once more. Our kids loved playing together, and we loved our girl talk. Marilyn was just such an ever-smiling, fun-loving, outgoing person. I do think that being best friends with her during that past year helped the ongoing transformational process inside me to continue. The persona I was developing was a mixture of the Sandy of old and the newer, more outgoing Alexandra. I was comfortable with Alexandra starting to become a more permanent part of who I was. I think a year earlier, the process didn't have the solidification it had by the early summer of 1973. My new overall personality had a more enduring feel about it, and I really liked who I was becoming.

It was during the early summer of 1973, while on a 5-minute alert shift, Lee J. stumbled across some travel magazines in the alert barn that someone had brought from home. He got to thumbing through them, and the idea of a second honeymoon vacation for us began to take shape in his mind. He came home and asked my thoughts about going on a second honeymoon-type vacation. Of course, I thought that sounded like a great idea.

I went through several of the magazines he'd brought home. Since we'd had such a great experience at Mexico Beach two years earlier, I started looking for the right place to take a beach vacation. Knowing what I had in mind, I started looking for out-of-the-way places. I wanted to go someplace with few people and a lot of privacy. One of the articles suggested an out-island of the Bahamas as a destination that fitted the bill for us. Honestly, I was looking for a place where I could experience the same freedom I'd had that last month we were in Florida two years earlier. Our destination would turn out to be Eleuthera in the Bahamas.

SECOND HONEYMOON
(Dare to Bare)

I stepped away from Lee J. and slowly started untying the strings to my top. I didn't let it fall away from me; I just held it in place to tease him. Then, off it came as I pitched it to him. From the last three days in the sun, my breasts were now quite tanned. He appeared spellbound. I slowly hooked my thumbs into the waistband of my bikini bottoms and pushed them down to my feet. I took one foot and kicked them off toward him. As I stood there before my husband, I was wearing only a mischievous smile. (Lee J. would later say it was more of a sexy smirk.) Standing before him completely naked in the sunlight on this beautiful beach was an awesome experience for me. What a feeling of love and contentment that I felt to be the wife of such a wonderful man. For me, it was a moment that took my breath away, and I think the same for him, too.

Then I told him it was time for him to lose his suit, too, so he did. Never before had we been in this situation where we both were "nekkid" on a beach 1,600 miles from home. ("Nekkid" became Alexandra's word for our state of undress.) We both thought it felt wonderful, and I'm sure we were a sight to behold. My only untanned area was what my bikini bottoms had covered. He took a long look at me for a moment and then told me that I reminded him of a cottontail rabbit—

a brown body with a white tail. I laughed and told him that he looked like one, too. He grinned and said I was probably right.

I was concerned that my previously unexposed area might be in for a sunburn unless I kept a lot of Coppertone applied. So I laid down on my towel and asked him to give me a full-body suntan lotion application. He did, but as always, he seemed to spend an inordinate amount of time touching places that really didn't need that much lotion. It had become our personal joke that he was really "bad" at applying any kind of tanning oil to my body. I've said earlier, he really was good at being "bad!" As you can imagine, this was more than a little arousing for me, especially the way he applied it to certain unnamed areas. He asked me to do the same for him. I did, and he had a similar arousal; however, his was far more evident than mine.

We strolled out to the shallow surf and decided to explore "our island." As we walked the beach both ways, I realized that this really was a small island. I'm sure we could have easily walked all the way around it, but we elected to stay close to the place where we had landed. I was ready to sun for a while, so we headed back to the spot where we'd left our bag and towels. He wanted some pictures to take home, but he couldn't very well take any for public consumption in my state of undress, so I donned his wet t-shirt and he snapped a couple of pictures. He did take several others during the day, which we have kept through the years.

We both spent quite a while just lying in the sun, talking about what we had experienced up to this point on our Bahaman adventure. Our consensus was that neither of us had expected all that we'd shared together the previous three days nor what we were experiencing at that very moment. Neither of us ever thought we would find ourselves lying naked together on a Bahaman beach, enjoying the pure pleasure of our sensual circumstances. We both thought our experiences these past four days on Eleuthera would be unforgettable; they certainly have been over the years.

After sunning for a time, I told Lee J. I needed to cool off, so I got up and walked out to the shallow surf while he stayed by the shade and just watched me. I knew his eyes were on me, and I was feeling giddy again, so I let what I was feeling show through my somewhat playful movements in the surf. He later told me I had a look of pure happiness on my face. The once bashful, shy girl that he had married nine years earlier was nowhere to be seen. He walked out to the surf to join me; he embraced me for a kiss. He told me he too was unbelievably happy. Of course, we both knew we were enjoying a euphoric state that would not last, but for the moment, we were both intoxicated by the sheer joy of being in our natural state together in such an extraordinarily beautiful place. We were a God-created couple, a loving man and a loving woman, being allowed to experience being in our own private "Garden of Eden," if only for a few hours.

How had I gotten to this wonderful situation I just described? After looking at the travel magazines Lee J. had brought home from the alert barn, I homed in on an article about the out-island of Eleuthera in the Bahamas. It sounded perfect for what I would like. Words like secluded, private vacation, and great honeymoon atmosphere all caught my attention. I told Lee J. about my thoughts, and he agreed to look into us going there. Without going into great detail, within a week, he said it was something we could afford if that's where I wanted to go. I told him I could hardly wait.

His suggestion was to drive to Idalou and have our parents look after the kids while we were gone for 6 days. We called and asked them if they would be interested in babysitting for us, and the answer from all of them was an enthusiastic "Yes!" So, we made plans to fly out of Lubbock on Monday and be back on Saturday. We had about a month to prepare, and in a couple of days, Lee J. took care of the reservations and plane tickets. Second honeymoon, here we come.

When I told Marilyn about Lee J.'s proposal, she was truly excited for us. I told her I had to get some new shorts sets made and that I needed a new bathing suit. I don't remember if it was Lee J. or Marilyn who said to buy something skimpy, and that's what I did. I'm pretty sure it was Marilyn's idea. When I look at the pictures we took from our time there, I think Alexandra must have bought it. The infamous pink bikini became the main part of my Bahamas wardrobe.

Of note! A picture of me wearing it on Eleuthera has circulated among the family through the years. It was shown at our fiftieth wedding anniversary party, and I remember one of the grandkids came by our table and said, **"MA-MA, you were hot!"** All they had ever known was Ma-ma, and the image they saw that night was far different than anything they had ever imagined. Such fun!

The thought of a second honeymoon was more than a little intriguing for me. We'd had a great time on our first honeymoon, but I felt like this was going to be something far different. First off, Lee J. was taking me somewhere that had a certain romantic charm that Galveston, Texas, did not have. The fact that our kids would be left behind, although they were in good hands, was both wonderful and worrisome. The mom part of me did not want to be so far from my children, while the wife and lover in me could hardly wait for a new adventure alone with my husband. The month I had to get prepared flew by, and we left North Dakota for the plains of Texas. We all made the trip just fine. We had a couple of days before we were to leave for the Bahamas, and we had a great time with both our families.

Monday came when we were to leave, and off we went. It truly was the second honeymoon time. The descriptions I'm about to relate are the vivid memories I still carry with me today. It's been over fifty years since Lee J. and I spent four wonderful days on the island of Eleuthera in the Bahamas. We've talked about our Bahamas trip over the years, and many of our family know bits and pieces of our adventure. This chapter is not a "tell all," but it is a "tell a whole bunch" narrative.

Also, I think some explanation is needed as to how the details of a time over 50 years ago can be so vivid to me/us. Well, what I relate here is a composite of my and Lee J.'s memories, and the results of many discussions between us as we looked in detail at the pictures that were taken during those four days. Most of the photos were taken by him with me being the subject. As you might guess, there were several where we were on a beach with me either topless or completely naked. They've never been seen by anyone but Lee J. and myself, and we will continue to keep them to ourselves. However, they did elicit some very vivid memories for both of us from that time long since gone by. As the story unfolds, it will be obvious that different things stood out for each of us, but when we put it all together, it was as complete as possible. There may be some slight errors about exactly when something occurred during those four days, but the reality that it occurred is real.

It had been nine years since Lee J. and I had married. We had not been alone together in a vacation setting during that time other than a single night here and there. The only exception being the two weekends during his days at OTS. I found after we got settled into our bungalow that this could be San Antonio on steroids for me, and I soon found out Lee J. felt the same way. Since our first honeymoon, except for the two weekends I just mentioned, we never had any time as a couple that remotely resembled what I/we experienced on Eleuthera. We would be empty nesters before we could have a getaway like this again.

So, on with my account of our second honeymoon to the island of Eleuthera in the Bahamas. The fact that I had to fly to get there was a bit of a downer for me. Here, I was married to a guy who flew for a living, and I hated to fly. I could get on an airplane, and I did, but I certainly did not enjoy it. The flight to the Bahamas was uneventful. We went from Lubbock to Dallas, Dallas to Miami, then out to Eleuthera. (I'll tell you now that the flight back **was** eventful, but more about that later.)

I think I should explain a little bit about Eleuthera. It's an island that is part of what is called The Bahamas. It's about 100 miles long and averages about a mile wide. It has miles of beaches and some tropical type of growth that one must go through to get from one side of the island to the other. It was a perfect getaway for a couple on a honeymoon.

The resort where we stayed was a series of triplex bungalows which weren't attached to each other. It was more like a series of small houses. It was quaint, it was quiet, and it was **romantic**. It was also basically empty. We were there during their "second season." When the brochure I read back in North Dakota said it had some very private beaches, that was an understatement. Add to that the fact that there were very few people at our resort made finding a private place quite easy.

The afternoon we arrived from Texas was spent doing a little exploring of the area near our bungalow. The beach by our resort was beautiful. The sand wasn't as white as the sand at Mexico Beach, it had a slight pink cast to it, but it was equally as beautiful. I remember thinking how perfect a place we had picked for our special time together. While we were exploring that afternoon, we decided we should rent a motorbike for the rest of our stay. We needed wheels to get around the area, and that bike turned out to be the answer. I loved riding on it with Lee J., and it could take us anywhere on the island we wanted to go. He figured out a way to strap our beach bag to it so we had our stuff with us all the time.

The next day, Tuesday, we planned to find our perfect (private?) beach and spend most of the day there. As I've related earlier in these writings, during my years growing up, my sisters and I had the summers to work on our tans. I grew to love "laying out." I tanned easily, but after leaving Mexico Beach, I'd had limited opportunities to enjoy that simple pastime. Marilyn and I had tanned together some during the month before this trip, so I already had the start of a pretty good tan. I was certainly looking forward to more of the same in the coming days.

I should interject here that this was a second honeymoon for us. Honeymoons, by their very nature, generally include a lot of passionate activity for most couples. I'll not give many details, but rest assured that Lee J. and I both enjoyed numerous episodes of carnal pleasures. That first morning was no exception. I'll move on from there.

We learned that the resort restaurant would pack a picnic lunch for its guests. So, we asked them to fix a lunch for us to take with us to the beach. We were getting ready to go, so I put on my new pink bikini. Lee J. had only seen me in it once, right after I bought it. When I put it on again that first morning, he said I looked amazing. Who was I to argue?

We hopped on our bike and headed out. As I've said, I loved riding with him on that thing (Does that make me a "biker chick?"). There were a few people on the beach by the resort, but now we had wheels, so we headed up the beach. We went maybe a mile or so, and found a beautiful stretch of beach, and **no one** was there. We'd found our spot.

As I previously expressed, I grew up getting a tan in our backyard with my sisters. I grew to love the feel of the sun and wind on my skin. I got my first taste of tanning topless in Florida, and I loved it. I mean, I really loved it. On our first day in Eleuthera, I found myself 1,600 miles from home with my husband in a honeymoon setting. I was having the same feelings I'd first experienced that Saturday morning back at Mexico Beach two years earlier.

After I'd laid out our beach stuff in the spot we had chosen, I asked him to put some Coppertone on my back. He said, "Sure!" He untied the strings on my top to do my back. When he had finished, I waited a minute, then I rolled over, and my top didn't. I reminded him, "Did you forget about my front?" He just laughed and began to apply the suntan lotion. I felt giddy; I felt almost intoxicated; I could be myself. I was Alexandra in this place. He wanted to take a picture of me there. He said we should take two, one with my top on and one without. I guess Alexandra was feeling naughty, so that's what we did.

We probably spent four or five hours there that day. We walked the beach a bit and never saw a soul, However, I did carry my top with me just in case someone appeared. **But really, on this spot of the beach, it was just us!** As you know, I love the beach just not the ocean. Again, I never got out much further than ankle-deep water because both Sandy and Alexandra are sissies. They can't help it!

I so enjoyed my day in the sun with my husband, but he didn't want to take a chance for a sunburn, so he wore a t-shirt a lot and never had any sign of a sunburn. I, on the other hand, saw my tan lines quickly start fading. We both used the Coppertone suntan lotion quite liberally, and I'm sure that helped. I was loving this freedom again that I'd first known in Florida. For me, this was taking "laying out" to a level I'd not known since those last weeks in Florida two years earlier.

We went back to the bungalow sometime mid-afternoon. It seemed that my nearly naked state all day had ramped up my husband's passion levels to the point that we found we both needed some relief. But late that afternoon, we took the bike and just went riding. There were roads all through the "jungle" to the other side of the island. Actually, "jungle" is a bit of a stretch. It was more of a lot of lush tropical growth with few trees. Now, we realized we had easy access to beaches on both sides of the island. By now, it was almost sunset, so we headed back to the bungalow. Alexandra had had such a fun day, and we still had three more to go.

The people who ran the resort suggested we visit a settlement nearby that was the result of a shipwreck back in the 1800s. It was a small island in itself and was home to folks who made their living fishing. They said it was a small community, but it did have a few gift shops and a sandwich shop or two. We decided to go the next day. To get there, we would take what they called the launch. It was a boat that could carry 10-15 people, and they made a trip twice a week during the time of year we were there. The next day would be the only time we could go, so we signed up. We were to leave around noon and return late afternoon. We would have the morning to ourselves and then go on the excursion that afternoon.

I told Lee J. the night before that I wanted to "sleep in" and have a late breakfast. (You are free to make any assumption you want.) He just shook his head, grinned, and said it sounded good to him. So that's what we did. Afterward, we had a late breakfast and still had plenty of time to go to the beach for a while. I asked him if we could go back to where we had been the previous day. I started to realize that he wanted to do whatever I asked if possible. He was so sweet. We quickly gathered our beach stuff and headed for our spot. Again, it was deserted, just like the day before. As soon as we got there, I removed the top of my bikini and spread out our towels. I laid down and asked him to put some Coppertone on me. It was obvious he thoroughly enjoyed what he was doing.

As I've said, I had learned to really love tanning topless. Part of it was the feeling of the sun on areas not normally exposed, but more than that, I loved providing my husband with the "special scenery" that he so obviously enjoyed. It was generally quite **evident** that he liked what he saw. Too soon, we had to get back to meet the launch.

We enjoyed the afternoon and the sights we saw were far different than any place we had ever visited before. The strangest thing about it all was the descendants of the shipwreck were all Caucasian, while the Bahaman population surrounding them was all Black. Lee J. joked with me and said they were like an Oreo, white filling surrounded by black cookies.

When we got back from our excursion, he asked what I wanted to do, and I said, "Let's go for a ride!" Like I've said, I loved riding that bike on the beach with him. We had hardly explored the east side of Eleuthera at all, so he took off through one of the "jungle roads" to get us over there. When we emerged on the other side, there was nothing but the beach and lots of it. He figured out the landmarks where the road emerged so we could find it again, and we took off. We quickly passed one or two houses, but for the most part, there was nothing but pristine, uninhabited beaches. He asked if I would like to spend the next day on this side of the island, and I told him that sounded great. To be honest, I had visions of spending most of the next day nearly "nekkid" on that beach with my husband; I just knew it would be a fun time. My unrepressed, giddy, elated mood was still with me. I'd never dreamed I would ever be in a place so isolated and so romantic with the wonderful man who was my husband.

Before it got too late, we headed back to the resort; Lee J. had no trouble finding the right road to the other side of the island, and it was near sunset by the time we returned. We ate supper, watched a beautiful tropical sunset, and then enjoyed sitting on the veranda of our bungalow as night fell on the most romantic place I had ever been. I was happy and content to be there with the sweet guy who was my husband. It had been such a great day and we still had two more to go.

I want to add something to my story right here. My husband had been and continued to be, for the rest of our stay on Eleuthera, the most attentive, the most romantic man he had ever been since our dating days. Anything I wanted or wanted to do, he did his best to make sure I got it. In the real world, couples can't always do that due to the distractions of everyday life. He told me later that he wanted this second honeymoon to be something we both remembered fondly for the rest of our lives. He succeeded beyond his wildest dreams. The main thing I wanted was to be with him, just us, and just us turned out to be no problem because there were so few people there at that time of year. Something about the setting we were in was bringing out the Alexandra side of me. Even before this trip, she was becoming a more permanent part of the person I was becoming. I'll admit she was the prime instigator for a lot of the sexual passion we shared during our days on Eleuthera. Yes, we made love a lot, but the trip was far more than that. Our closeness as a couple and the bond we shared was certainly strengthened during this time. You just don't forget things like that.

Now, for the rest of my story about the last two days on Eleuthera. We made plans to spend Thursday on the east side of the island. We "slept in" again that morning and had a picnic lunch from the resort restaurant packed for us again. We loaded our beach stuff and lunch and headed for the east side of the island. We probably weren't more than 4-5 miles from the resort, but it seemed further because we had to go through the "jungle" to get there. Lee J. found the place we had located the day before, and once more, not a soul was to be seen.

It was apparent we were alone, so I found a spot to spread out our beach stuff. This time, I took my top off with no plans to put it back on until we had to leave. Again, I had such a joyous feeling of freedom. Alexandra was here, and neither Lee J. nor I wanted to be in any other place. He sat down in the wet sand and just watched me as I waded in the ankle-deep surf. I'm not sure what he was thinking, but the look on his face was one of total approval. Oh, how I loved my guy in that moment. The part of me (Alexandra) that loved tantalizing him with what he referred to as "interesting scenery" fully emerged that morning.

I soon laid down on my towel and had him put some Coppertone on me. I loved the feeling of what he was doing. He told me he was really "bad" at applying suntan lotion to me, and he did seem to give an excessive amount of attention to places on my body that ordinarily I wouldn't think needed that much protection from the sun. He was just so "bad!" This was a great start to what was going to be a great day. He was still afraid of getting too much sun and getting sunburned, so he put his t-shirt back on. I continued to relish my "laying out" for a while longer.

He suggested we move up to a spot that had some palm trees for shade and break out the lunch we'd brought, and that's what we did. After finishing the lunch, we decided to take a walk along the beach. The beach was pristine; there were no signs of anyone having ever been there. (I'm sure that was not the case.) I kind of lost myself as we started a long, leisurely stroll on this isolated stretch of beautiful beach. We were probably a half mile or so from where we left the bike and our stuff. He casually mentioned that if we met someone right then, I didn't have my top with me. I don't remember what I said to him, I just remember I didn't care. It was like I was drunk on some kind of euphoric drink. I was certainly loving this unrepressed, unrestrained side of Alexandra. He was, too!

We spent the whole afternoon just talking, sunning, or walking in the shallow surf. We would splash enough water on each other to cool us both off a bit. It wasn't very hot, but there also wasn't much breeze, and the water felt good. Alexandra was certainly in her element. It was getting toward late afternoon when we thought we should head back to our bungalow. We gathered up our stuff, and reluctantly, I had him tie my top back on. It had been a wonderful time alone with my husband. It was a day I've never forgotten. Little did I know the next day would be even more unforgettable.

When we got back, we were both tired, and Lee J. left for a few minutes to see about "something." That something turned out to be a surprise for me. As he watched me earlier that day, he thought as much as I seemed to love being nearly "nekkid" with him on that beach, I just might like to spend a day totally "nekkid" with him.

The something he had gone to check on was the possibility of us going somewhere close by that was totally private. What he found out was amazing to both of us. The manager told him to talk to his guy at the marina about a place where someone could go when they wanted complete privacy.

So, of course, my husband went down to the marina to talk to the guy he had been told to contact. He found out that there was a small uninhabited island about a 15-minute boat ride from the marina. Lee J. asked him what the charge would be to take us there tomorrow morning and pick us up in the afternoon around 4:30. I don't remember what the price was, but it was reasonable. He wanted a third of the money to reserve the time and the rest when we got back the next afternoon. He came back to our bungalow to see if that was something I wanted to do.

When he told me where he'd been and what he had found out, my only reaction was, how do we know he'll come pick us up? He explained that the guy with the boat to rent was associated with the resort, and this was something they did quite often, so this was not an unusual request. Even with my normal skepticism, Lee J.'s explanation sounded reasonable.

Alexandra was 1,600 miles from home on her second honeymoon and being nude on a private beach with her also nude husband sounded exciting and fun. With no hesitation at all, this new version of Alexandra said, "Let's do it!" Lee J. went back to the marina and reserved the boat for the next day. It was a Friday I will never forget.

When he returned from the marina, we just hung around the resort until bedtime. As we talked, he told me he had promised himself that he would not pressure me at all when he asked me if I would want to go on such an outing. He **hadn't** pressured me; the decision was completely Alexandra's. In fact, Alexandra was more than ready to spend the day au naturelle with her husband. Later, he confessed that this was something he had always wanted to do too.

Of course, the next morning, we "slept in" again. We had breakfast and then ordered another picnic lunch from the restaurant. We gathered up our stuff, went by the restaurant to pick up our lunch, and showed up at the marina a little early. Our boat and driver were ready, and we were soon on our way. Fifteen or twenty minutes later, we were arriving at "our island." On the way out there, Lee J. asked the driver how often he brought people out for a day like we were doing. He said 2-3 times a week during the season, but we were the first in a couple of weeks. As we unloaded, he asked what time we wanted him to return. Lee J. told him 4:30.

As we waded through the surf, I looked around and thought this was more than perfect; it was idyllic! We took our beach bag and towels up to a shady area under some palm trees. We stood there together as we looked around, again, I couldn't help telling him how romantic this place was. He had decided there was no place on Eleuthera that didn't seem romantic to me. I was once more becoming intoxicated by "our island's" environment, just as I had been on the other beaches we'd enjoyed during our previous days there.

It was at this point in our activities that day that the narrative of this chapter began. We were now completely naked with each other in a "Garden of Eden" environment that was breathtaking for me. I think there's something about me becoming physically naked in such an environment that allows me to also become psychologically naked at the same time. That's the only way I can explain the freedom I felt that manifested itself in my actions that day there on that beach. It was the same sense of freedom I'd felt the three previous days on Eleuthera, but that day, I would experience even greater freedom to be who I felt I'd truly become. It would all happen on the place we would come to call "our island."

By now, it was well past lunchtime when I told Lee J. that I was hungry. We got out the lunch that had been packed for us, and as we ate it, I off-handedly remarked that I had never been on a nude picnic before. He had to admit that neither had he, especially with such a beautiful lady. That was a nice little compliment, he added. Little did we know that in years to come, when we had our own backyard pool, we would enjoy such on a regular basis. The time we spent that day on "our island" unexpectedly would start a trend for us.

Later that afternoon, as we were enjoying a walk in the shallow surf, I suddenly took off running. He didn't follow me. He later said he just wanted to watch my untanned tush as I ran, splashing water everywhere. I ran 25-30 yards, stopped, and turned around. He says he didn't remember saying anything, then suddenly I started running back toward him, yelling, "Arturo, Arturo." Then it came to him; I was reenacting a scene from an old movie we had seen where two lovers see each other on the beach and run towards each other with their arms open wide. The woman is yelling, "Arturo, Arturo!"

He told me later that he couldn't help but watch me again, only this time, his gaze was riveted to the rhythmic swaying of my undulating breasts. He spread his arms as I got near, thinking I would leap into them. He then expected we would kiss passionately (that's the way the movie went), but none of that happened!

Suddenly, I went off script and veered around him. Instead of having my naked body to embrace, he had nothing. I stopped just past him, and as he turned around, I walked back to him, laughing. I held my arms out, and this time, we did embrace, and I gave him quite a passionate kiss.

I then took him by the hand and led him back to where our beach towels were laid out. I suppose earlier, I thought we might end up making love on that beach at some point, but neither one of us had mentioned it to the other. However, the kiss I had given him as we embraced there in the surf left no doubt about what I wanted. By now, it had become a mutual desire. The passion we had enjoyed during the past three days had been wonderful, but this time, it would be different. We were on an island 1,600 miles from home; we were alone on a beautiful, deserted beach; we were both naked and had been the entire day; we were both now fully aroused; we were a loving man and a loving woman. This would be no fantasy in our minds; this would be real.

I'll leave the details of our lovemaking to your imagination but suffice to say, we both knew that this experience on a deserted beach in the Bahamas would probably be a once-in-a-lifetime experience for us. As we became one and began to move together in a kind of primal dance, he was in no hurry, and neither was I. We savored every touch; we savored every kiss; we savored the tenderness we both felt for each other. Never had the term "making love" been more apropos.

Afterward, we lay there in silence for a while. I got up first and walked out to the water's edge. He told me later it was quite a sight for him to watch me. He said that he'd always thought God's most beautiful creation was "woman." He went on to say that he marveled at me, the beautiful creation that was his wife, standing at the shallow water's edge, clothed only in the sunlight from a blue Bahaman sky.

Soon, as I stood in the ankle-deep surf, he got up and walked out to me, held out his hand, and we slowly started to walk down that beach. Not a word was said between us; we were both deep in thought. My thoughts were of the nine years of our marriage, the love we had shared, the three little girls we had made, and the way he had become someone who tried to please me on every level. My mood was one of deep contentment.

He says his thoughts were similar, and it's almost embarrassing to write his words about me, but they are so precious. He said that he knew he was a blessed man to be able to share a life with such a beautiful woman and an even more beautiful person. (He was probably still euphoric from our lovemaking that had just happened, but I hope not.) I'm tearing up just writing this.

All this was an experience that I still remember vividly, even today. Some things are truly unforgettable, and what we had shared that day was truly unforgettable. Finally, he broke our silence, telling me how much he loved me; he embraced me and kissed me once again, but this time very tenderly. I responded in kind.

We still had an hour or so until our water taxi was due back. Neither of us wanted this day to end, but soon it would. We sat down in the shallow surf just to look about and soak in the beautiful environment we had enjoyed that day. There was one exposure left on the film in the camera, so he had Alexandra pose as demurely as possible while sitting there amidst the surge of the shallow water. It's one of my favorite pictures from those experiences.

Neither of us could quite believe what had happened during these last days on Eleuthera. What follows is a paraphrase of the things I related to him as we sat there at the water's edge. I told him that four days of freedom on those beaches had changed me forever. I felt like Alexandra would become integrated as a permanent part of my persona for the rest of my life.

I told him that the release of Alexandra had been a process that had taken place for me over the entire length of our marriage. I felt that I had made a large leap forward especially during our last days in Florida, but also during our time in Great Falls and Grand Forks. Especially in Grand Forks since I became best friends with Marilyn. She had been quite an influence, but now, after four days in the Bahamas, I'd felt more freedom to be my new self each day. I was sure that I was finally free. Alexandra was now a permanent part of who I was and who I wanted to be. I assured him I was not going to do something inappropriate at the wrong time, but I would have no problem with Alexandra being around when the circumstances seemed appropriate for her to emerge.

He gently shook his head and whispered, "Wow!"

Too soon, we heard the sound of our ride back to the resort. We reluctantly donned our swimsuits and gathered our beach bag and towels. As the boat pulled up, we climbed over the side and headed back for our last night in the Bahamas. He watched me as together we took one last look at "our island." What a memory we had created in those hours there. It was a time neither of us have ever forgotten. Writing this account of those days on Eleuthera and especially the hours we spent on "our island" has only intensified my memories of such an unforgettable time. I hope through the words I've written on these pages, I've conveyed how special our week in the Bahamas was for both of us. Sandy/Alexandra was never quite the same after that week. She was complete.

Upon returning to the resort, we got ourselves ready for the flight back to the States the next day. That night, as we gathered our thoughts about our honeymoon time on Eleuthera, we agreed that there were two main takeaways from our time there. The first was that Alexandra was now a permanent part of who I was. The four days of unrestrained freedom on the beaches of Eleuthera had wiped away the last vestiges of my adherence to childhood rules I had subconsciously taken into adulthood. A more outgoing part of my nature was now fully incorporated into my personality.

Alexandra would be with me on many different levels throughout the years. Alexandra helped me develop my skills as a salesperson working for Daddy and my brother-in-law, Dan, in years to come. I subsequently applied those skills to running the Window Gallery, which I described earlier. The kids soon learned that my Alexandra persona was not one to trifle with. Alexandra could be a parent with skills outside the box. They much preferred their mom in her Sandy mode as opposed to her Alexandra mode.

The second takeaway from "our island" experience earlier that day was the discovery of how much we both enjoyed being naked together in an outdoor setting. It would be many years before we had any similar opportunities again. After we built our pool in 2004, we would enjoy regular skinny dipping in our own backyard pool. On most days during the summer, even now, we enjoy a skinny dip in the West Texas sun. It all goes back to the time on "our island" that week in the

Bahamas.

The Bible says that everything has its season and our season on Eleuthera was ending. We were to fly out the next morning on Out Island Airways. Oh Boy! No sleeping in the next morning for us; it was time to go. But first, I must explain a little bit about Out Island Airways, our mode of air transportation back to Miami. Most of what I tell here is from my pilot husband. (Okay, a lot of it is.)

They were a **small** airline serving the out islands of the Bahamas, of which Eleuthera was a part. Their airliners were old Convair piston-driven aircraft. They had seen their better days twenty years before. Our flight out from Miami with them was uneventful. We got off at Eleuthera which was their first stop of a four-hop route. Returning to Miami, again, we were the first stop of the same four-hop route which means we had two stops before we headed to Miami. The airplane would probably hold 40-50 people. There weren't more than 10-15 on it when we got on in Eleuthera. It would have many more by the time we headed to Miami on the last leg of the route.

Lee J. has told this story for years, and it's quite funny the way he tells it. I'm going to give you the short version. We made the two scheduled stops before we started the last leg back to Miami. Lee J. was concerned since the left engine was running really rough the whole time, and it failed completely when we were headed to Miami, but we were directly over Nassau. The pilot made an uneventful emergency landing on one engine, and we were transferred to a flight on the old

Braniff Airways. We got to Miami safely and made our connection to Dallas. Though I was a nervous wreck, I did get my wits about me and made the flight back to Lubbock okay, but it was stressful.

We changed planes in Dallas and got back to Lubbock mid-afternoon. Everybody was there to greet us, and those three little girls of ours were a sight to see for this mother's eyes. We had been gone since Monday and had made memories we would never forget, but I was so glad to see our kids again. I don't remember whose house we went to, but someone commented on the nice tan I had gotten while we were gone. Little did they know just how much of me was now tanned, more than just a little. Not until now have I ever told the full story of our four days in the sun on our second honeymoon.

Upon our return, the Sandy of old was not gone; she was just a more complete person. As situations changed in my life, I knew Alexandra was there to help me. She was now a part of the mixture that was my new and more complete personality. He said that he had come to love the new Alexandra part of me. We left Eleuthera with some great memories and a deeper bond in our marriage than ever. In later years, he would tease me and ask if Alexandra was going someplace with us that might resemble a date. I would generally ask, "Do you want her to go?" His response would be, "Well, she _is_ a fun date, and the scenery she provides is beyond comparison." His date was generally with some version of Alexandra. We were both happy.

We stayed 2-3 more days with our families, and then it was time to head back to North Dakota. Real life had returned! We had an uneventful but long journey home. Lee J. went back to his regular schedule, and the kids and I went back to no particular schedule. School would be starting in a few weeks and Angie would be in kindergarten.

A Farewell to Arms

Upon our return from the Bahamas, Marilyn and I continued to see each other daily. We started lying out together again. She just laughed when I showed her how tan my boobs were and filled her in on some of the details of our wonderful time on Eleuthera. She just laughed and said what memories you both must have. Having a best friend right next door was one of the best things I have ever experienced. Having her to talk to was always a treat, but being able to share with her the intimate details of our trip was really special. I've only had two best friends in my life, and Marilyn was one of them.

Alexandra had certainly made the trip back to North Dakota after our Bahamas adventure. It wasn't one single thing I could put my finger on, but her persona definitely had given an extra dimension to my personality that previously wasn't there all the time. Marilyn definitely had a role in the process of incorporating Alexandra into my new and more complete persona.

Grand Forks was very pleasant during the summer months, and I tried to stay outdoors as much as possible. Having been through the two previous winters in Montana and now North Dakota made me appreciate warm weather more. I'm not sure where we came up with four bicycles of such varying sizes and configurations, but we were quite a sight as we all rode around the housing area as a group. My bike had a buddy seat on it for Marnie. I tried to stay in shape and since Marnie was the kid at home, we would go for rides around the base housing area during the school day. We have one picture of Marnie sound asleep in that buddy seat before I got back to the house on one trip. What a dumpling she was. Life was good, but change was soon in the air.

In August, once more, we had West Texas visitors. This time, it was Mother and Daddy, along with Kathy and all of her bunch. Chuck had done the driving, and again, Mother loved the trip. They stayed for almost a week and we saw all the sights. It was a good time for all of us, but again, it was time for them to leave about the time school was to start for both Julie and Angie.

In September, Lee J. found out he was to take an airplane (an F-106) to Reese Air Force Base for an open house and a Thunderbirds performance in late October. He was excited to get a chance to show his kinfolks and others what he had been doing for Uncle Sam since he joined four years earlier. I, on the other hand, was not so excited because he would be at home, and the kids and I would not. But this really was part of his job, and the scheduler knew he would like this assignment. Little did we know how important this trip would be for Lee J. personally.

He was originally supposed to go solo, but on the day of departure, one of his younger flight members, Pete Anderson, was assigned to go with him. (It's a complicated story as to why this happened.) They got into Reese around noon on Saturday before the open house on Sunday. When Pete shut down his airplane, a mechanical issue cropped up. They reported the issue to the 460th FIS maintenance control and were told to forget about it for now. They were instructed to call maintenance control back on Monday, who would then sort it out. Raymond had bought tickets for the Tech game that afternoon and the plan was for Raymond and Gwen to take both Lee J. and Pete to the Tech football game. That's what they did, except Pete decided he'd go sit in the student section. He thanked Raymond for the ticket and said he would see them tomorrow at the open house.

Lee J. had asked him to stand the static display. That was fine with Pete and that's the way everything went. When Raymond, Gwen, and Lee J. showed up the next day, Pete had found himself a companion. The companion was a real "hottie coed" he had met the day before. (Lee J. said she "was in 'luv' with Lt. Pete.") Lee J. and Pete set up a time to meet the next morning to figure out what to do about the maintenance issue on Pete's aircraft. Raymond took Lee J. to Reese the next morning. The short story was that a big inspection team had shown up at the 460th and they weren't concerned at all about the airplane with a problem 1,000 miles away in Texas. They told Lee J. to send Pete home in his aircraft, and for Lee J. to stay in Lubbock until they contacted him later. Later turned out to be Thursday.

When I found out Lee J. wasn't coming home on Monday, I was upset. What I didn't know was that the next three days would turn out to be the most special three days Lee J. ever spent with Raymond. They worked together on some kind of old hunting vehicle Raymond was fixing up. Their conversations during this time were probably the most heartfelt and meaningful they had ever had. Raymond was so proud of Lee J., and for the first time ever, he told him so face to face. He told Lee J. how much he loved me and our girls. Lee J. said his dad went on and on about how special he thought I was and that Lee J. had really picked a winner when he married me. Lee J. had no way of knowing that these conversations were the last he would ever get to have with his dad. A little over three weeks later, Raymond passed away of a massive heart attack.

They finally resolved the issue they had with the aircraft Pete had flown into Reese. He got home midafternoon Thursday. Little did we know how our lives were about to change. After Lee J.'s return from Lubbock, our life returned to normal. There had been no hint from either Raymond or Gwen about his heart issues.

On the Sunday before Raymond died on Saturday, November 24, 1973, Lee J. left with some of his squadron mates for some kind of deployment to Tyndall for five days of special training. Friday night, after a week of training, there was a party and Lee J. went to bed late. Somehow, he had gotten a message that his dad was going to Methodist Hospital in Lubbock on Friday for some tests. The next morning, he called the hospital and asked to be connected to his dad's room. The operator paused and then came back with this message, "I'm sorry, sir, Mr. Everitt expired this morning."

So, that's how Lee J. got the news that his dad had died. He then called me to inform me of the news. I really don't remember many of the details of how he got from Florida to Lubbock or how I got from North Dakota to Lubbock with three kids in tow. I know I had to change planes in Minneapolis and Dallas. I had Julie and Angie holding on to my coat while carrying Marnie plus a huge, fully stuffed diaper bag. Julie was so good and helped to make sure Angie didn't let go. Somehow, we made it to Lubbock on Sunday. If these events had happened four years earlier, I'm not sure I could have done it. Being an Air Force wife has a way of teaching a person how to take care of the world. It didn't hurt that I had a helper inside me named Alexandra. She made me push aside the anxiety I knew could overwhelm me at any time and just do what had to be done. I had come a long way.

I hardly remember the next few days; it was such a sad time for both Lee J. and me. He had told me the things that Raymond had said three weeks earlier about me and the kids. He was so complimentary about the kind of wife he saw in me for his son. I was deeply moved. They were especially precious after learning of his death. It was such a sad time for everyone.

Gwen tried to put on a face that everything would be alright, but she was not alright. How could she be? She'd just lost her soulmate. I remember nothing about the following days before we went home on the weekend. The flight home was better than the flight down to Texas a week earlier, but Grand Forks was having a blizzard and the flight could not land. Therefore, they diverted us to Jamestown. After landing, we were loaded onto a Greyhound bus and spent four hours driving all the passengers back to Grand Forks. There were no cell phones or any easy way to call to tell everyone we were all right. My daddy was climbing the walls by the time we contacted him when getting off that bus at the Grand Forks airport at 3:00 am.

The next few days were a blur for both of us. Lee J. was worried about his mother and also the Vega family. They were the Hispanic family that had worked for Raymond for more than twenty years. Someone at the squadron put a bug in his ear that he probably would qualify for a hardship discharge. The fact that he was facing a reassignment within the next year and rumors were swirling around what that might look like made him check into it. It was a possibility.

He came home and asked me what I thought; I immediately knew that I wanted to go home. Looking back now, I realize what a tough decision this was for him. I think he convinced himself, wrongly, that he could walk away from flying and be happy as a farmer in Idalou, Texas. **He was wrong, really wrong!** (More about that later.) He made the decision to apply for the hardship discharge but would not know if he would take it until after the Christmas break when we went home. He needed to know if he could keep renting the farmland from the Cone's. He needed to know if he could get the farming operation financed. There was so much to figure out over the Christmas holidays.

We came home for Christmas and told Gwen what we were thinking, and of course, she was fine with it. My folks were the same way. While there, he made an appointment to meet with Mr. Cone and his daughter. He told them he would like to rent the farm where he grew up and pick up his dad's operation. After some questions, they agreed to rent the farm to us, and we could live in the old farmhouse located where Lee J. grew up. He sat down with his dad's banker, and they also agreed to finance the operation for him the same as they had done for Raymond. If the hardship application went through, we would move back home.

When we returned to Grand Forks, they were still processing his discharge application. It was approved, and we found out we were to become civilians on January 15th, 1974. I was happy to be going home, but it was hard to say goodbye to Marilyn. I had never had a friend like her before, and only once since that time would I ever have another friend as close as we were. Leaving Grand Forks was to be somewhat bittersweet. But life goes on, and so did we.

I thought about who I would be after returning to live where I had grown up. I felt sure the person I had become would stay with me even as I went back to my roots. But it was going to be interesting to see how I would handle being a much different person living back at home after those years away.

Down on the Farm

During the spring after our return from North Dakota, I asked Lee J. about buying a pool membership in the Idalou Pool Association. He thought it was a great idea. Someone had offered to sell us their membership, so we bought it. I knew that the girls and I would use it a lot during summer. The pool opened shortly after the school year ended, and we all showed up. I decided to wear my pink bikini from our Eleuthera trip the year before; it elicited several comments, but everything I heard was positive. It didn't hurt that I had been working out at home, and I had the start of a good tan.

Even after all these years, I've never forgotten that one of my old classmates from high school commented that if she looked like I did, she'd wear that pink bikini, too. I definitely appreciated the fact that everything that was said was complimentary. I really hadn't given much thought about wearing that particular swimsuit that day, but as I looked around, there were no other young women my age wearing swim attire quite like what I had on. Having been away from Idalou for almost five years, I realized that my comfort level was now far different than it was before our Air Force years. It would not have made any difference even if the comments were **negative**; they would not have changed my attire one bit. The only persons I felt the need to please were myself and Lee J., and I liked the way I looked. He told me quite often how beautiful he thought I was. Alexandra had certainly made her statement, and I was extremely comfortable with what I had on. My persona (Alexandra) at the pool that day bore evidence to everyone that the girl who had left for the Air Force five years earlier was not the girl who had returned to Idalou in 1974.

In the years since Lee J.'s enlistment into the Air Force, we both had changed. When we left, I was a young woman and mother who still dealt with anxiety issues and who, at times, could be extremely shy and bashful. I returned as someone who, as an ex-Air Force officer's wife, could push all that stuff aside. I came home as a person who could operate independently of her husband if necessary (I emphasize the "if necessary" part). Lee J. and I were still a team, and both of us wanted it that way. He loved that Alexandra was now a permanent part of my personality. I probably looked about the same (just slightly older) to those who had known me five years before, but I was now different, and I liked who I had become.

When we got back home, we stayed with Gwen until she closed the deal on a house in Idalou. As soon as she moved, we had our stuff delivered and began life at what came to be known as the "farmhouse." I found I loved living out in the country in that old house. It had been remodeled a few years earlier and was very comfortable. The Vegas lived right next door and the interaction with our kids was great. Pifi, their mother, loved fixing the girls' fresh tortillas, and I had to caution them not to bother her all the time asking for them. Julie and Angie would send Marnie over to do their dirty work. She was the "designated beggar" for them. Pifi treated them like her own kids. Maybe better! I think our three little girls were quite a welcome change for her after dealing with her four younger boys.

Since we moved back in the middle of the school year, getting the kids enrolled in school was a priority. Julie was in the third grade when I enrolled her in school at Idalou. She was in Mrs. Steen's class, but there was no public kindergarten in Texas as there had been in North Dakota, so Angie went to her Aunt Barb's private kindergarten. After a few days, I got a note from Mrs. Steen that she could tell Julie was a "bright little girl," but she was behind the class since she didn't know her multiplication tables. I almost went into a panic. We had a crash course at home, learning them all. Lee J. used to kid me about her learning them all one night. It didn't quite happen that way, but it didn't take long before she knew them completely.

The other funny thing was the school called and asked if they could enroll Julie as a "migrant." This carried a little stigma with it, and I was concerned that she might be treated differently by the school, but that was not the case. As we had moved in from another state, the school could get extra funds for migrant children. However, Barry, one of her more obnoxious classmates, somehow found out about it and started teasing her about being a migrant. Julie came home to me asking, "What's a migrant?" She would tell me later that he was just being "Barry, the turd," but technically, she **was** a migrant.

The next year, Angie was also enrolled as a migrant. We've laughed about this for years. Welcome to Texas! Both Julie and Angie would ride the bus to school, and Barb would pick up her kindergarten kids (including Angie) in their station wagon in the morning and take them back to the school for the bus ride home in the afternoon. I didn't worry about the bus ride for Julie and Angie because all the Vega kids rode the same bus, too. They kind of looked after the girls. Let's just say there was a mob that got on or off the bus at our house.

That left just me, Marnie, and the dogs at home. I loved being home with Marnie. My thoughts about her were, *this child makes me tired. She's so busy being happy, she doesn't want to sleep!* After dealing with the previous two kids who liked to sleep, especially in Angie's case, Marnie was exhausting. She slept fine at night, but during the day, she cared nothing about taking a nap. I loved her dearly, but she could wear me out.

Looking back, I'm not quite sure why we had so much company during those years. Of course, we saw a lot of family once we moved back. That old "farmhouse" just screamed comfort, and I tried to provide a very relaxed environment for those who came to visit. We had a lot of family that came out to visit along with others our age from the church. Also, we went by Mother and Daddy's house a lot and with Barb's kids close by, there generally was a party going on. My reconnection with my sisters was really good for me, and PaPa was glad to have all his chickens close by once again.

While things involving the family were going really well, 1974 was turning out to be a very dry crop year. It was not a good year to start farming. Lee J. had trouble getting the crop started, and it was stressful on him to say the least. He tried to keep a good attitude about everything, but it wasn't easy. By June 15th, he did have a decent crop started and felt somewhat better about things, but he had no passion for what he was doing. It would eventually get better, but 1974 was hard for him.

He found himself feeling so out of place because most everyone that he associated with in the farming community expected him to be the same person that he had been five years earlier. He felt little connection with them, and he most definitely was not the person he once was. He explained it to me one day by saying that most of the guys he saw regularly thought the center of the universe was the Idalou water tower. For them, that might have been true, but for my husband, it was not. He had done and seen things they could not imagine, nor for that matter, most of them would not have wanted to imagine. He knew that for the good of his family (us), we were in the right place, but that hardly eased his transition back into civilian life. He really missed the close-knit camaraderie of a fighter squadron. He said he didn't know how, but someday, he would fly again. That prophecy turned out to be true.

I required some adjustments on my part, too. I was coming back home as a person who was quite different than who I had been before our Air Force years. I came home as someone **unwilling** to embrace all the restrictions and rules I had once lived under. I'm not talking about my mother's rules. I'm talking about the accepted mores of my hometown. I liked wearing clothes in the summertime that exposed more skin than was the norm for other young women my age there in Idalou. My time in Florida, Grand Forks, and the Bahamas had changed me. The fact that I thought nothing about wearing my pink bikini to the Idalou pool probably let most everyone know that my ideas for my summer fashions were not the norm. I didn't think my summer clothes were provocative; I was adequately covered, but I did bare a lot of skin, primarily because I was strictly looking for things that were comfortable. There definitely was a defensive element involved.

I soon found out that wearing apparel that was somewhat minimal was necessary if I was to have any chance of being comfortable living in the "farmhouse." It had one old evaporative cooler that was not very effective in keeping that place cool on a hot summer day. I still had some of the shorts and halters I'd made during our time in Florida three years earlier and made good use of them. The no-bra look was in fashion during the seventies, and during the summer, I never wore one unless it was absolutely necessary. No bra, no shoes, that was me. Had I not returned to Texas with Alexandra as an integral part of a new me, I would have had a very uncomfortable summer.

My love for sunshine and a nice tan fit right in with the fashion choices I made. My experiences tanning topless and completely naked were something I wanted to continue if possible. Early on, I really started thinking that I might have an opportunity to get an all-over tan during that first summer we were back. It turned out to be the same for all the summers to follow for as long as we lived in the old "farmhouse." I grew to love how I looked in a head-to-toe tan.

One of the advantages of living in the old "farmhouse" was its privacy and seclusion during the summer months. After school ended and summer vacation started, Pifi and all the Vega kids went to work as hoe hands in the fields. They would leave early in the morning and return in the late afternoon. That left me and the kids having the place completely to ourselves during the day.

By the time summer came, I had started lying out some. From previous chapters, it's obvious that I had a real love for being outdoors and enjoying the feel of the sun and breeze on my skin. The memories of our time on the beaches of Eleuthera were still fresh, and I realized that with Pifi and her kids at work in the fields, the "farmhouse" was indeed a very secluded place.

In our house full of girls, there was a lot of incidental nudity in our day-to-day life. The kids would gather in the bathroom while I was taking a bath. There, they had a naked lady in the tub who was a captive audience for all their girl talk. I used to laugh and say I didn't think I'd had a completely private bath in all the years the girls were at home. As I related in an earlier chapter, my sisters and I did the same with Mother as we were growing up. I suppose I was just carrying on a family tradition with our girls. The point is that they were used to seeing their mother naked a lot, so me laying in the backyard sunning without a stitch on was nothing special.

I have to admit I had become somewhat vain. Anyone who has read my previous words knows that Lee J. would tell me that I was the most beautiful woman he'd ever seen, and he told me so quite often. I loved to hear him say that and I guess I believed him. I liked staying fit and having a nice tan. The "farmhouse" was so isolated that I found that I was comfortable lying out topless even when he wasn't around. He wasn't surprised when I told him that I really would like to sunbathe naked. However, I wasn't totally comfortable doing that unless he was close by. He told me to give him a little heads up, and he would try to be around; I did just that. When he could, which was a lot of the time, he'd make it a point to be around for me. It seemed most convenient for him around lunch time. That worked for me, too. (He would tell me the lunch time ambiance I provided was fantastic.)

I think I should give some explanation about my desire for sunbathing sans my suit. I had found that after our time in the Bahamas the previous summer, it boiled down to two reasons, possibly three. The first was that I got a very even, deep tan that was totally smooth. For me, that meant I could wear anything I wanted and never have to worry about tan lines I so disliked.

The second reason, and equally important, was the intoxicating feeling of the sun and the breeze on my completely bare body. It was a feeling that I found addictive the previous summer in the Bahamas. I found I had brought some of those feelings to Texas with me. Upon reflection, it's obvious that the addition of Alexandra to my persona had a big part in my tanning desires. It was an easy way for me to prove to myself and Lee J. that Alexandra was certainly a part of who I had become. I was aware that my feelings were unconventional, but I didn't think there was anything wrong or immoral about being naked around my family. I assure you my husband didn't either; he loved it.

If there is a third reason, it involves Lee J. He has always been a very passionate person; he's had a passion for flying, music, and me—all of me, not just the sexual side. He's told me for years that he loved seeing me, not just my bare body, but the person I was as his wife and as a mom for our kids. **He's had a passion for all of me!** I found I really enjoyed providing my guy with the visual images of seeing me sunbathing nude there in the backyard of the "farmhouse."

In looking at most of the pictures that were taken either at home or with my family, I generally had on shorts and a halter. That was what I had gotten used to wearing during the summers during and after our time on the beach in Florida. I was aware that what I wore was not the norm for my sisters, but neither they nor my mother ever said anything other than to compliment me on how cute an outfit was that I had just made. Since I was not overly endowed in the boob department, I went without a bra a lot because previously, my choice of summer wear was definitely not out of the ordinary, especially in the military community from which we had just moved. For the three previous summers, I had grown quite comfortable with my summer wardrobe choices, and I had no intention of changing anything now just because we had moved back to our old hometown.

I loved to sew and continued to make a lot of the clothes for myself and the kids. On most days, I would put on one of Lee J.'s tee shirts to wear around the house. They were light and very cool. I was in no way an exhibitionist; I was just a young farm wife wanting to stay as comfortable as possible. For those who have never experienced living in a house "cooled" by an evaporative cooler, imagine an environment of high humidity and just slightly cooler air than the outside ambient air temperature.

So, most of the summer clothes I made for myself required no bra. To sum it all up, I made outfits that were in **fashion, cool, and comfortable**, and I thought I looked **really good** in them; my husband surely told me I did. Alexandra **liked** the fact that she did not conform to the norm for most of my contemporaries. I've come to realize there was a bit of a rebel in her. It would stay that way for the four years we lived in the "farmhouse."

I knew Lee J. was not having a smooth transition moving back into the civilian world. During our Air Force years, he'd always had both of his passions in his life in a big way. That summer in 1974, he said he felt incomplete. One of his passions was completely missing, and he had been wrong, so wrong, in thinking he could walk away from flying and be okay. I suppose he was okay, but just barely. His passion for me and the kids was still there for him, and I did feel so sorry for my guy. During our Tech Village days, we used sex as a coping mechanism. I tried to help him during this time in this area of our life. It was certainly not something that was hard for me to do, and I did try to make our lovemaking often and intense for him. I hated to see him sad, and our lovemaking did seem to help him cope.

The fact is that the old "farmhouse" had some real charm about it, and one of the things that charmed me most was that we slept with the windows open during the summer. Making love with Lee J. by those open windows sometimes seemed like we weren't inside the walls of the house at all; it was almost like we were outdoors. I suppose it was similar to the feel of our time on that beach in the Bahamas. It made our lovemaking all the more special as I listened to the wind rustle through the leaves of the old elm trees just outside. Even after almost ten years of marriage, I loved seeing our bodies being bathed in the moonlight streaming through those windows after our lovemaking was done. On many a summer night, afterward, we would cover ourselves with only a sheet, yet there were other nights when it was especially warm that we chose to lay naked, covered only by the warm night air. Yes, my guy was coping with a situation he found to be less than perfect, but I think he did find some solace in making love with me in such a unique atmosphere that was our bedroom in the old "farmhouse." I knew I was a blessed woman to be able to share my love with this man!

Being back home allowed us to begin taking the kids and ourselves back to church on a regular basis. Bro. Kendrick, who had performed our wedding ceremony, was still the pastor there. We found that the Sunday School class we were in had a lot of couples and we befriended them. Larry and Patti Work and George and Becky Woodward especially come to mind. There was the social aspect of going to church, which we enjoyed a lot. We soon realized that our new friends liked to come to visit us at our home. I tried to be a great hostess and felt like making that old house just scream comfort. We had a lot of really great, entertaining times out there. The kids were soon involved in the programs the church had for their age groups. Soon I was making a lot of trips to Idalou for our kids' school and church-related activities. Though Lee J. was missing flying, being back in our hometown community allowed us both to see our kids start enjoying some of the same things we enjoyed as kids when we grew up in the Idalou community.

I was somewhat coerced into broadening my horizons by joining a bowling league. I was to be on a team with three of Lee J.'s old classmates from high school. I was a horrible bowler, but we had a lot of fun together. One of them made a comment recently that I thought was worth mentioning. It was that the sweet, shy Sandy that they had known years earlier was now capable of comments that would have them laughing on the floor. I suppose Alexandra had made it to the bowling alley, too.

It's obvious that Alexandra had found her way to Texas, in what I've revealed so far in this chapter, but as the kids grew older, they began to realize that their mom could have a somewhat Jekyll and Hyde personality. In later years, they would laugh and say that it was better not to cross the line that caused the Alexandra side of their mother to emerge and replace sweet Sandy. There is one story in our family lore that illustrates this perfectly.

I call this the **"Get out of the car!"** story, and it concerns what some might call parenting outside the box. I call it "Alexandra parenting." I have always said that I was sometimes hard on my girls. My mother, being my mentor in this regard, was hard on me and my sisters, and I followed her example when our kids came along. Let me set the scene. Of course, we were living in the old "farmhouse." I made countless trips to and from Idalou since that was where all their activities were. One day, as we were headed towards Idalou, the following events took place. I was driving, Julie was riding "shotgun," and Angie and Marnie were in the back seat. Like many of these occasions, the noise coming from the back seat was not loving, sisterly, quiet conversation. The sisters were **fighting**. At one time, I had been able to swat them from the front seat if necessary, but lately, they had learned how to stay out of my reach. So, unable to administer corporal punishment, several verbal warnings were issued. The last one being, "If y'all don't stop that fighting, I'm gonna stop this car and put both of you out, and you can walk the rest of the way to town."

This warning went unheeded (short pause). "Alexandra" stopped the car beside the road about three miles or so from Idalou. As soon as the car came to a stop, she told our two youngest daughters, "**GET OUT, NOW!**" Slowly, the door opened on the right rear of the car, and two petrified children got out of the car and huddled on the side of the road. Alexandra told them that they had to walk in the bar ditch the rest of the way. By this time, the two wannabe fighters from the back seat had fallen in love with each other and were huddled together as they started to walk. The car which their mother, Alexandra, continued to drive, moved slowly along just ahead of the two young delinquents. Meanwhile, Julie had lost her crap and was hysterically screaming from the front seat, "Let them back in!" The two younger outcasts have now started thinking they love each other **a lot,** and maybe they underestimated their mother's threat to make them walk the rest of the way to town.

After a short distance, Alexandra stopped the car and asked if they thought they might complete their journey without any more fighting. She was assured that they would not fight anymore. That turned out to be a lie because they fought off and on for years to come. But for that day and the near future, a threat to stop whatever it was that was irritating their "Mom," Alexandra, was sufficient to get order restored.

Though Lee J. and I have laughed about this incident for years, the girls did learn that their mother's patience could wear thin, and there was a line they did not want to cross that would cause their mother's alter ego, Alexandra, to take charge. The adage "actions have consequences" was true when she took over a situation, and there certainly were consequences when Alexandra emerged. Sometimes, those weren't found in any standard parenting help manual. She had some very different out-of-the-box discipline techniques. I still laugh every time I think about that and my kids. They also vividly remember that day and can recount the incident verbatim even today.

As our first year out of the Air Force was winding down, Lee J. gathered the crop; it was adequate, considering how hard it was to get it started. He had learned a lot and felt much better about another year in the farming business. He certainly still had no passion for being in the farming game, and he missed not being involved in aviation in some way, but he was coping. He knew that his decision to leave the Air Force was the right one for me and the kids.

The next year would find him expanding the farming operation by acquiring another farm in Floyd county to work. He had Lupe and his family move to the new farm, which was a better situation for them. The house he could provide for them was far bigger than the one they were living in next to the old "farmhouse" where we lived. He pretty much let Lupe be his own boss on the two farms he took care of up there. Lupe liked that.

The "farmhouse" now had even more seclusion and privacy. However, the increased seclusion and privacy had both its positives and negatives. The kids missed playing with the Vega boys and eating Pifi's tortillas. I missed having two babysitters next door, but I really loved the seclusion, especially in the summertime. For the next three summers, I spent a lot of time without my clothes as I sunbathed in the backyard. I suppose I had gotten somewhat careless because I actually got caught once and never knew about it until years later. One of Lee J.'s hunting buddies came by to look at a dog box he had made, which he'd left in the back yard. I obviously had fallen asleep while sunbathing that day. He saw me but quickly turned and left without ever waking me up. It was years later when he told me about it. His only statement was that he was momentarily stunned seeing me lying naked there in the yard. I'm sure he got quite an eye full since I had the time and the inclination to stay very fit during those years and Lee J. told me repeatedly that my all-over-tan was stunning. Once we moved, my opportunities for such were drastically curtailed.

The kids were doing well, I was loving our life and Lee J. was coping. We had been home for four years now, but things weren't good for us in the farming business. The crop year of 1977 was horrible. If it could go wrong, it did. In an attempt to get a little financial relief for the next crop year, Lee J. tried to renegotiate his rental agreement with the Cones. The rental agreement with them had not been modified since his daddy's first crop in the late forties. They did not budge. Lee J. said it was their attitude more than anything else that really pi$$ed him off. He said, "Their overall 'attitude' lit his fire." As cordially as he could, he told them they could kiss his A$$, and he would be gone when we got the current crop harvested.

As soon as he got the crop harvested, our days of living in the old "farmhouse" came to an end. It had been quite an education for us in many ways. By cashing out what had been his daddy's farming operation, we were left basically broke, but we got out of the farming game, not owing anyone anything. He **was** unemployed, but I knew he had skills, and this might be his chance to get back into flying. It would turn out that way.

In November, we rented a nice four-bedroom house just north of Idalou. Now, we had a place to live, and a new era in our life was about to begin. In our four years living in the "farmhouse," my new persona had served me well. Both Lee J. and I liked who I had become and who we were as a team. We were both sure that we were starting something new that would be great.

Though our future was unsure, the one thing I was sure about was that any worries I'd had about reverting into the Sandy of years gone by had been quelled. For sure, Alexandra had remained a part of me as we returned to Texas. I know there were some who were somewhat shocked when they realized that I was nowhere near the same person I had been before our years in the Air Force. The subconscious rules I had been adhering to five years earlier were now long gone. I was now who I would be for the rest of my life.

Transitions, Again

As 1977 ended, I found myself living in a very nice house (I'll call it Donna's house) on a pavement, 1 ¾ miles north of Idalou. My husband was unemployed and wasn't sure of his future. All the kids were in school now, and we could use the money, so I decided to go to work. I don't remember exactly how Daddy and Dan came to offer me a job at the Kirby store, but they did, and I took them up on their offer. I was to be the bookkeeper, answer the phone, and take care of the front if Dan or Daddy weren't there to handle it. I loved it. Mother was close by if one of the kids needed something. She came in real handy a lot. More than once, they called her if there was some controversy among my children (fighting). There are all kinds of stories among my children about how to keep red marks on one's body really red until Mama Gracie arrived. (OH, my!)

Lee J. worked doing some carpentry during the winter months, and with my job, we were making it. We both knew that this was only temporary for him, but his future was still a bit murky. He learned that the GI bill would pay 90% for type ratings (an FFA rating for a specific type of aircraft). He knew that to fly again he had to get current. That just meant that he had to have a recent history of flight experience. He decided that he could get current again by going to Dallas and getting a type rating in a Learjet. The GI bill would pay the vast majority of the cost. He did that in late February and came home as a freshly current Learjet pilot with no job, but he was current as a jet pilot. He had a lead on a job in Midland, but he wasn't too keen on going down there. Neither was I. He decided to talk to Arthur Newton again about possibly flying for him as an ag pilot. They had talked around the edges of such a thing since we came back to Idalou after leaving the Air Force. That day in March of 1978, when he walked into Arthur's office, would change our lives forever.

The short version of this story is that he and Arthur went flying in Arthur's Super Cub (I don't know what that is for sure!) for about an hour. At the end of the flight, Arthur thought enough of his abilities that he said he'd hire him if Lee J. could become insurable in his spray planes. Getting to be insurable would require a couple of months of ferrying old spray planes to California for the local Piper dealer. So, that's what he did. By the first of May, he almost had enough of the right kind of flight experience to be insurable in Arthur's ag planes. Arthur decided to take a chance and let him start flying his planes **uninsured**, for him to get the remainder of the flight time he needed for insurability. It was toward the end of May when Arthur called one day about lunchtime and said a big customer had turned in a large number of acres that needed to be sprayed. He asked Lee J. if he wanted to help. Are you kidding? He flew with Arthur one afternoon and the next morning, he came home with a $700 check for his work the previous afternoon and that morning. That was a lot of money back then for about a day's worth of work flying. I was flabbergasted! Lee J. was overjoyed! **He had found his flying** niche in ag aviation.

I had settled into my role at the Kirby store, and I loved it. I did the books, answered the phone, and I soon got to interact more and more with the customers coming in. Daddy and Dan were both comfortable leaving the store to me and Manual, our repairman, if they both needed to be gone for a while. Daddy still loved to load up his vehicle and just "go across the country and see the people." That was the element of the business he loved the most. Dan took care of the outside errands for the store during the day sometimes, and that left the front of the store in Alexandra's hands.

Meanwhile, "back at the ranch," things were getting on track for Lee J. He loved his new career in ag flying, and he loved working for Arthur. He had been told that Arthur could be hard to work for, but he and Lee J. worked together just fine. They had known each other for years, so it wasn't like they were strangers trying to get to know each other. Lee J. always said in later years that he was much better at being an Indian than being a chief, and he loved being Arthur's Indian. Arthur told him later that they had had the perfect season to break in a rookie. They never got too busy, but there was always some flying to do every day. Lee J. already knew most of the customers and their farms and seldom made any mistakes. Arthur seemed very satisfied with his work. Since Arthur had two airplanes, they flew a fair amount together. Lee J. told me that the formation flying skills he was taught in the Air Force made it very natural for him to quickly be proficient when two airplanes were flying in tandem in the same field. I used to love watching them spray a field together. It literally was like watching an aerial ballet. I will say again that I hate flying for myself, but watching them work two airplanes together was fascinating, and my husband was certainly having fun again in his life (happy husband, happy wife and vice versa).

Our relationship never suffered while he was farming after we left the Air Force, but I always knew there was something missing in Lee J.'s life and now he felt complete again. I knew full well that the something he was missing was flying steadily again. The two greatest passions in his life have always been **me** and flying airplanes. He has told people repeatedly that getting out of the Air Force took him away from high-end military aviation, but it was his choice at the time. He left the Air Force to put **me and the kids** ahead of him. He knew it was the right choice. He just didn't know how he was going to get back into flying. It took a while, but it happened. I would say that the type of flying he was doing did carry some risk with it, but he obviously was becoming very good at it and flew as safely as possible as that first season progressed. In fact, he never had an accident during his entire aviation career. Little did we know that me working in retail sales and him flying spray planes would be our life for the next twenty or so years.

Since we had returned to Idalou upon leaving the Air Force, we became regular church goers again. No alert shifts and deployments to make every week a bit different as far as the schedule was concerned. There was a social aspect as well as a spiritual aspect that went with being regulars at the First Baptist Church in Idalou. Most of our friends came from our age group from the church. I, in turn, started teaching at Sunday School in the junior girl's class. I loved it and taught for years to come.

Since I was working full-time with Daddy and Dan, my time with the kids was primarily at night when we were all at home. One of the things that was a carryover from my growing up years was talking to Mother while she took a bath. She was a captive audience for me and my sisters, especially since our house had only one bathroom. The same happened to me when we lived at the farmhouse. I generally had company during my bath time, just like my mother did. The bathroom in Donna's house was much larger than the one at the farmhouse, and now I had from one to four guests (my husband now included with the kids) while I was in the tub. We would get to talking, time would pass, and I would have to reheat the water ever so often. When I finally did get out, I felt like I probably looked like a wrinkled prune. I think these "conversation conventions" lasted as long as some of our kids were still at home. Though most families had conversations around the dinner table, at our house, some of the best conversations within the family turned out to be around my nightly bath time. I know the visual images of these "conventions" might be considered a bit weird by some, but I have nothing but very fond memories of those times. Everybody had something to say and got to say it to the naked lady in the tub.

I know our kids think I was hard on them at times, and more was expected from them than what some of their friends had to deal with, but my mentor in matters like this was my mother. She had her ways, and in the case of Barb, Brenda, and me, a lot was expected. I went to work after they all were in school, and I couldn't coddle them. They had to handle some things on their own. Mama Gracie had to be the referee much too often, but all in all, I think it worked out well. I believe it was during the time of this chapter when Marnie earned the title of "The Little Sister from Hell." She was what she was!

The spraying season for 1978 had drawn to a close, and Lee J. was now officially on board with Newton Spraying. As I stated before, Arthur was pleased with his work, and he had a "seat" (ag pilot slang for having a job) for next year. We talked about our future and what we would like to do. We both wanted to buy or build a home of our own. We offered to buy Donna's house. But she thought that one of her kids might eventually want to come back to Idalou (One of them eventually did.), so she didn't want to sell her house. Lee J. especially liked the location we had not far from town and got the idea of contacting the owner of the land adjacent to "Donna's house." He approached him about selling us a tract from his land next door to where we were living. We had enough cash from the spraying season to afford to buy a tract if we could find one. Our world was about to change again.

Lee J. called Jerry (the owner) and asked if he would sell us 200 front feet off the pastureland located next door to where we were living. He said he'd have to think about it and that he would get back in touch. Sure enough, a couple of weeks later, the phone rang one night, and it was Jerry. He not only would sell us the 1 ½ acres we wanted but was going to plat off the entire pavement frontage of the pasture in which our tract was located. There were to be five additional tracts in addition to ours. We would start the trend to build north of Idalou (trendsetters?). A deal was finalized and soon we had a place to build our dream home.

Lee J. started doing carpenter work again during the winter of 1978-1979 and I continued to work at the Kirby store. Life was good for us. We knew we could use Lee J.'s GI Bill eligibility for financing, so we started planning to build our house after the 1979 spraying season (if it was as good as 1978). Lo and behold, that's what happened.

We started construction on the house in February of 1980 and moved into it in August of that year. It would not be long afterward that we would purchase The Window Gallery and my career as a business owner would begin. The earlier chapter, called "Minding My Own Business," picks up my journey as we move from the "farmhouse." It recounts my life in 1978 and my subsequent career as a businesswoman. It does not give much in the way of my life as a wife and mother of three daughters. My purpose here is to elaborate on my time as a mother of teenage daughters while at the same time running a successful business. What a busy time that was.

TEENAGE GIRLS, OH MY!

I wrote earlier that I'm sure the kids sometimes thought I was too hard on them, but they were so pretty, smart, and talented that my expectations for them were very high. It wasn't my nature to brag about them, but looking back, I think I should have! I should have told them how special they were to their dad and me. I don't regret pushing them, but I do regret not telling them how much I loved them and how proud we were of them. I just wasn't wired to express my feelings to them so openly because my model for raising kids was my mother, and she was not a communicator of her feelings to me and my sisters. We just knew what she expected; I wish now I hadn't followed her model so closely in this area. I've talked about the "conversation conventions" associated with my bath times. I always enjoyed those times, and I felt our communication lines were open, but I didn't tell them about my deepest feelings during these times. Maybe my words on these pages will convey that message. I hope so!

I must be quite honest here. Lee J. and I have needed to talk to each of the kids at various times to help us sort out the timeline of a lot of events during these years. I hope we've got it close to right. The 80s were the busiest, most intense of my life. Being a businesswoman, a mom, and a wife can be quite a juggling act. We helped Julie get her hardship driver's license when she was 15 so she could get her sisters to where they were supposed to be when I was at work. I'm afraid I dumped quite a lot of responsibility on her. Though she was playing basketball, she was still her sisters' chauffeur, the grocery shopper, and cook for all of us at times. I look back now and think, "That was quite a load for her." Her response to all of this was that her responsibilities during this time helped her develop her independence; she learned how to grocery shop, how to cook, how to clean, and, in other words, how to run a household when she got one of her own. She told us later that it gave her a great amount of confidence in this area.

She reminded us of the time when I broke my hand. I confess, I was trying to hit Lee J. He had been teasing me about something, and I hauled off and semi-playfully swung at him. To defend himself, he threw up his elbow, and I hit my hand on it when I swung. (I know that was stupid!) While my hand was in a cast, I had to enlist Angie to fix my hair. It was inconvenient for both of us. Julie's other takeaway from these times was that "Marnie was a brat, and she was sure of it." I probably would have to agree with that to some extent. More about that shortly.

I mentioned that being a wife was also a part of my life. I knew that Lee J. was more than proud of me for the way I ran the store and handled the kids. But honestly, he was close to **worthless** when it came to understanding his girls. He had no mentor in that area when he was growing up, and he was sadly lacking any skills in understanding teenage girls. Plus, he tended to fly off the handle at them at times and go into a tirade of some sort (out of frustration, I guess). They laugh now and give their impersonation of one of his tirades. They say his vocabulary generally included phrases like "sick and tired," something about "attitude adjustment" to go along with the ever-popular "y'all's' bitchin'." All this was performed while he was wearing his standard uniform of "whitey tighties." I can't help but grin when I say this, but I must confess that I witnessed some of his performances, and the kids' version is pretty much spot-on. Many times, he would ask me, "Is what's going on back there normal?" Each time I assured him that it was, he would roll his eyes and say, "Maybe you should handle it," and so I tried. As the decade wore on, more and more, he deferred to me because he knew I was far better at handling the situation than he would ever be. Bless his heart!

No matter the time of year, one or both of us was always busy, but we always seemed to make time for each other to be by ourselves. Thank goodness, he insisted on having our master bedroom on the opposite end of the house from the girls, and yes, there was a lock on the door. There was something about locking that door that could shut out the busyness of our lives. The click of that lock invariably let the passion of our youth sweep over us once again. The sexual passion we had for each other from the early beginnings of our relationship never seemed to wane when we were behind our bedroom door. At least for a while, the craziness of our world would calm, and the bond of our love for each other would be renewed. Though the lives of our girls seemed so chaotic, there was so much change for them; behind that closed door, there was no change for Lee J. and me. We remained as one.

That has never wavered.

In 1982, Arthur decided he was going to sell the spraying service and asked Lee J. if he was interested in buying it. He was, but we certainly did not have the money. Lee J. needed a partner with some money if a purchase was going to be possible. After coming up with some possibilities, it came down to this. My daddy offered to buy in as a silent partner with Lee J., and his brother, Tootie, offered to redeem his teacher retirement and buy in as a participating partner. Lee J. decided to go with his brother. He just liked having him close by. He had missed him during the Air Force years and when we came back to Idalou. It was a complicated transaction, but they got it done. So, the 1982 spraying season would be the first as Everitt Aerial Spraying. It turned out to be a disastrous spraying season. It was a dry year, and there were few bugs and little defoliation.

They had picked the worst of times to buy out Arthur. The stress on Lee J. was significant, and it was made worse because he had gotten his brother involved. He always had a kind of "take care of little brother" mentality, and the whole situation weighed on him a lot. However, the next year would be a big one, and things got better in a hurry. I was mostly on the sidelines, watching since I had my hands full getting The Window Gallery really going.

Julie and Robert Dowdy started dating in 1981. Robert was destined to be our first son-in-law, but it would be 1984 before they married. Meanwhile, we had a family to take care of. As I've talked about earlier, I had put a lot of responsibility on Julie since she was the oldest. Part of it was dealing with her little sisters.

One of the funny stories in the family lore involves Julie's boyfriend, Robert. Marnie came in one night very upset because we wouldn't let her be chosen as an all-star for her little dribblers team. She came in and went storming through the house. Robert said something quite innocuous, and she yelled, "Shut up, Robert!" then stomped to her room and slammed the door. Julie was furious! So, I went back to Marnie's room and scolded her that Robert didn't deserve being yelled at like that; go apologize to him. She went back to where they were and crawled into Robert's lap and sobbingly told him she was sorry. Her getting into Robert's lap to apologize also greatly irritated Julie. I'm sure both Julie and Angie sometimes thought that Marnie was the little sister they never wanted, and they aptly dubbed her the "little sister from hell." I admit, she was a handful.

When the 1980s started for Lee J. and me, we had one in high school, one in middle school, and the other in elementary school. They all seemed to be involved in everything. They all took piano lessons, so there were lessons and recitals to attend. All the girls, at one time or another, were cheerleaders; all were involved in athletics, from basketball to track. They were all a part of the youth group at church. Viewed from my perspective now, it makes me tired to think about the chaos of those days, but at the time, it was just our "normal." I'm thankful that we were able to give our girls a stable environment in which to live through their teenage years.

Although, there was a question just how stable their daddy was during these times! (Just kidding!)

I should mention that I never had to worry about their grades. Julie was the valedictorian of her class, and Angie and Marnie were in the top 10% of their classes. Lee J. and I were both so proud of each of them. I don't remember ever having to push any of them to keep their grades up. It was just understood that good grades were expected.

After Julie graduated in May of 1983, she enrolled in Texas Tech, for the fall semester and lived at home but moved into the dorm for the second semester. She did help me some at the store in both '83 and '84. She and Robert were an on-again, off-again thing until he left for the Navy in September of 1984. I guess absence makes the heart grow fonder. Soon, the letters were flying back and forth, hot and heavy, and the first thing I knew, we were planning a December wedding for her. Julie had just turned 19 a few days before the wedding.

Robert was scheduled to leave on a six-month cruise in March after their December wedding. So Lee J. and I flew to Virginia to drive her back home for the time he was on that cruise. While there, we got our tour of the USS Nimitz, and Lee J. loved it. He always said that the Nimitz was a great big boat, but for an Air Force guy, it was a little-bitty airport. Julie also remembers that I made Lee J. stop at every roadside park between Virginia and Idalou for me to pick up pinecones. So, what's your point?

When she came home with us, she moved into an apartment in Lubbock with Robert's sister, Sharon. She got a job as a Kelly girl, working for a commodity broker in Lubbock. Julie's routine was to come home for Robert's long cruises and go back to be with him when the ship was in port. She was able to get some additional hours of college credit during these times of separation.

Finally, Robert's commitment to the Navy was to be up in May of 1987. He got out then, and they came home and moved in with us. It made sense for them to move in with us since Julie was pregnant and due in September. Robert had gotten hired by the FAA but wasn't to enter Air Traffic Control school until September. So, with three months to kill, Robert needed a job, and the spraying service needed hangar help. Julie was going to need some help with a new baby, so we had a nearly full house again for a few months.

Angie had graduated from high school in 1986 and started to Texas Tech in the fall. She lived in the dorm and **fully embraced** her college experience. She worked several different jobs during her college days. She even worked for me some, but that would be later.

The year 1987 turned out to be full of events for all three of the girls. Some of great magnitude, others not so much. In Marnie's case, it was the year she diagnosed herself with a retarded left hand and begged to switch from piano lessons to voice lessons. We found a highly recommended teacher who agreed to take her on, and the rest is history. She became quite an accomplished singer.

Angie had her first date with her future husband, Steve, in April of '87 but didn't start dating him for real until October.

There was some story about having to dump his current girlfriend so he could seriously date Angie. In the meantime, she dated a lot of different guys. Lee J. has kidded her for years about the story of her having two dates in one night; she did admit it required some pretty tight scheduling to get away with that. Her second date with Steve must have sealed the deal. They would be married in 1989.

As I said earlier, Julie was pregnant when Robert was discharged from the Navy, and the subject came up as what our grandparents' names were to be. I know Lee J. was just being a smart Alec, but he told everyone he wanted to be called "Mr. Everitt." All the girls, including me, told him that not only would no kid be able to pronounce it, but it was just a really stupid idea. We would assign him a name, and he would have no choice in the matter. So, we named him Pop, and I became Mama (pronounced Maw-Maw). It's worked out well.

Julie made us grandparents in September of '87 when Matthew Lee was born. That little boy rocked my world. When Julie left the hospital with him, they came to our house. Robert was leaving to go to Air Traffic Control School in Oklahoma City around the end of the month and there was no other place to go. I loved it. "Matty Matt" lived at Mama's house for a while. I don't remember the exact sequence of the back and forth from Oklahoma City to Idalou, but it was after Christmas before they permanently moved to the Metroplex (Dallas/Ft. Worth). I was so attached to that little boy that I cried when they left. I think it was almost a grieving process.

Robert was determined to get back to the Lubbock tower as a controller. It would be several years as he worked the FAA employment system to be able to get an assignment to Lubbock. He finally did get that assignment and one set of my chickens came home to roost. (I should add that he was not trying to get back to be close to his mother-in-law. LOL!) His goal was to give his family the small-town environment he enjoyed growing up. He wanted the same environment for his boys, and he eventually got it.

As the decade was drawing to a close, Angie and Steve set a wedding date in June of 1989. Once again, I was the mother of the bride and was in the middle of all the planning. I was in my element, and I loved every minute of it. Thank goodness the store was making plenty of money. I spent what I felt was necessary to make it all perfect, and it pretty much was. As the '80s drew to a close, I found myself in new roles that I had never experienced before. I was now a mother-in-law. I had gained two sons-in-law, and I loved them both. Lee J. and I both thought Julie and Angie had picked the right young men to be their mates.

I also assumed the role of a grandmother. Julie and Robert had made us grandparents, and I fully embraced my new role as Mama. That became my name to everybody. We now lived in Mama's house. Mama was letting Pop live there, too, but it **was** Mama's house. Of course, we were not through. Both Angie and Marnie would fill our "quiver" even more. Our "quiver" would eventually swell to nine grandchildren, six boys and three girls. They would be spread out over nineteen years. I had become a grandmother at the ripe old age of 41. I was loving my role as Mama.

Our first five grandchildren were boys. I would soon learn that I was not quite prepared for these strange creatures called "grandsons." Rough and tumble activities were unfamiliar to me. In that same conversation, Lee J. also told me our girls never smelled like wet puppies, either. Nevertheless, I loved them dearly.

It was my role as Mama that started a transition for me. As the decade of the 1990s began, I found myself embracing my role as Mama more and more while preparing to eventually leave my role as a businesswoman in retail sales. By 1990, I had proven to myself what I could do in the business world. I had also proven to my daddy that I could succeed in the world without a college degree. He was so proud of my accomplishments. His words quoted earlier said it all when he told Lee J. and Dan that Sunday, "That Sandy is something, isn't she?"

I had also emerged from Lee J.'s shadow to become my own person while operating The Window Gallery—he had encouraged me every step of the way. I don't think many men would/could have done that. But now my heart was moving me in a different direction.

We made the decision to close the store in '91 and let it wind down as I ran it from home. I felt a mixture of sadness and relief. I was sad to leave something I had put my heart and soul into yet relieved to be out from under so much pressure. Juggling the demands of the store, the demands of being a mom and now a grandmother was wearing me down. Add to all that, I was still the wife of a great guy I loved deeply. Closing the store was like the analogy I have used so many times earlier. I was the bird who had been let out of its cage. I soon embraced my new freedom and quickly learned to enjoy it.

My Sandy/Alexandra character had accomplished so much in the decade of the 1980s. As I look back, I'm sure I could have never handled everything I did without finding my true self. My true self turned out to be the result of the melding of the original Sandy and the previously hidden persona of Alexandra. Together, they became who I truly was, and I really liked who I was.

THIRD HONEYMOON, ARE YOU KIDDING?

It was in the spring of '93 when Lee J. and I decided we needed a vacation; it was to be our first vacation since our trip to the Bahamas twenty years earlier. I wanted it to be a road trip to the southeast United States. I summed it up to someone by describing it this way. "We left Idalou and went south until we hit I-20. We headed east on I-20 until we ran into the Atlantic Ocean. We made a left turn, went up the coast and hit I-40 at Raleigh, North Carolina. Then we took I-40 to Amarillo, then I-27 back to Lubbock, then Lubbock to Idalou." Pretty simple, huh? It would be around 3,500 miles.

We were gone for a little over two weeks, and we both thought it was wonderful. It was just the two of us again, and it was a special sixteen days. We had been married for almost 28 years at the time, and from the look on our faces in the pictures from that trip, we could have been on our first honeymoon. Lee J. wanted me to do all the planning. He told me he really didn't care where we went, all he cared about was that I got to do exactly what I wanted to do. I had done most of the planning twenty years earlier for our Bahamas trip, and what a trip that turned out to be.

We both had been so very busy for so long that he just wanted me to feel completely free to go and do whatever I wanted to do. Before we left, I decided to call it our "Third Honeymoon." Our two previous honeymoons had included a lot of sexual passion. When I told him I was planning our "Third Honeymoon," I knew he wondered what exactly I had in mind. He shouldn't have worried about anything along those lines.

I've related earlier, Lee J. had always said that spending the night in a motel with Alexandra was always a fun date, and the scenery she provided was spectacular. Though we weren't as young as we once were, we had over two weeks of "motel nights," and trust me, Alexandra (the uninhibited version) was going on this trip. I told him I wasn't about to leave her at home, and I certainly didn't. He'd learned long ago to always try to get a room with a king-size bed (Alexandra really loved a large **playground**), and that's what he did. Basically, Sandy ran the daytime sightseeing portion of our trip and Alexandra was in charge of our "motel nights." What a wonderful combination we were to enjoy on this trip. For a couple who had been married for almost thirty years, the sexual passion we both enjoyed was almost unbelievable. No, we didn't make love on a beach like we had done twenty years earlier, but I made sure that my guy and I had many memorable "encounters" during those sixteen days.

Lee J. said he witnessed me become as giddy as I had been on the beaches of Eleuthera. I was happy to my core, and it was so much fun just being "us" on that trip. We loved the great sights we'd seen, the places we'd been; we loved the talks we'd had about any imaginable subject; we loved the laughter we'd shared from time to time, but we especially loved the passionate intimacy we shared during those "motel nights." For over two weeks, there were no distractions from the outside world to prevent us from looking forward to letting our passion overtake us again night after night, and that had certainly been the case. Alexandra had definitely left us with great memories of those night times in the South, but after sixteen days and fifteen motel nights, we pulled back into Idalou. It had been a honeymoon in every sense of the word. The main thing was we had over two weeks of just being "us."

Each day had become a new adventure. We both knew we'd rekindled our passion for each other's physical touch, and we'd found that it was as strong as ever. It's been thirty-one years since that trip, and as we talked about the material to include in this chapter, my memories of what I've just described were exactly the same as his. Great times make for great, long-lasting memories. The whole trip became one of those memories.

When we returned from our "Third Honeymoon," we were truly just the two of us once more. We were officially empty nesters. However, our nest may have become empty, but the tree where our nest was located was full of our nestlings on its nearby branches. That fact would keep the Mama side of me quite busy in the years to come.

In Closing

I'm leaving this writing at the point where Lee J. and I had just returned from what I called our "Third Honeymoon." I think this is the proper place to wind down this story. We'd just completed a sixteen-day trip where we had rediscovered being just "us." We would return to our empty nest as just a couple once more. The journey that I've related in these previous pages had started almost thirty years earlier when we were just "us" for the first time. That was during our first honeymoon, right after we were married.

As I've thought back to those early times when we started out as just the two of us, the journey that I've been on has been quite transformational, and I like who I've become. Lee J. has told me that the girl he fell in love with is certainly still a part of who I am even today, but she has become far more multidimensional. She is more complex.

The title that I chose for this book, Releasing Alexandra, says a lot in and of itself. The implication is that my transformation was not so much a complete replacement of who I was as much as it was the liberation of a part of me which initially, I was completely unaware even existed. Over time, I came to realize that part of me, named Alexandra by Lee J., had been there all along but had been buried deep within my psyche.

Lee J. and physical distance from home were the key

components of my transformation. Over time, as he embraced my newly found persona and I found myself in the right environment, Alexandra was released. She was free, and with her, I was free. Upon leaving the Air Force and returning home, I found that Alexandra was a permanent and fully incorporated part of who I was and who I would remain to be. The journey to release her has been quite the ride! I hope you've enjoyed my revelations.

She's still alive and well today as I write these words. She is definitely a part of who I am even now in my golden years.

FOREVER'S AS FAR AS I'LL GO

By Lee J. Everitt

We ended Sandy's memoir when we returned from our Third Honeymoon to the southeast in 1993. I'm writing this as myself for all who have read her memoir's words about her early years. I'm giving an update on our lives today (late December 2024). Our clan now numbers twenty-seven, with another little one in the "oven." Rumor has it that a couple more marriages may be on the horizon. Sandy truly embraced her role these last thirty years as Mama for this crazy bunch of characters we call our family. That's the good news.

Now for the not-so-good news! It's been a little over two years since Sandy was diagnosed with early Alzheimer's disease. She was experiencing some cognitive decline and wanted to know the **truth** about her medical future. The diagnosis was not unexpected, but it was unwelcomed. There is no cure, only treatments to slow down the progression of the disease. She is currently on the latest Alzheimer's treatment, and I do think it is probably helping.

She's still my Sandy/Alexandra, but not quite the same as the person she was in her early years of discovery that we've just chronicled. These days, I'm her caregiver, and we still have wonderful times together. She's still really sharp when it comes to things long past. Short-term memory is an issue.

We started working on her autobiography two and a half years ago and finished it in a little less than a year. It was primarily for our family. There were over 150 pictures included, and it was her life story told chronologically from her birth up to the date we finished it in early 2023. We wrote it together, with me as her ghost writer. We've done the same in this work. I took an enormous amount of material and notes from her autobiography and incorporated it into *Releasing Alexandra*. She has gone over every word several times in this memoir and confirms it is accurate. She can still tell me if something isn't quite right and help me edit and fix it. She's a stickler for her story to be accurate.

Our writing of this memoir has helped her cognitively. As we go over each chapter, it refreshes memories that have started to dim for her. She couldn't do today what we did when we started her autobiography two and half years ago. Even now, we generally read something from it several times a week. We keep a copy lying on the coffee table in our family room. It helps her freshen those memories of days long past each time we read them. Her spirit is remarkable. "Alexandra" surfaces and jokes about her disease and helps me to smile even when I don't feel much like smiling. What a spirit!

In our wedding vows, we promised to love each other in sickness and in health. We've done that through the years and also today. Part of my passion for her has been to be there for her in good times and bad. Through these years, she has always been there for me during some of the ups and downs of our life together. I remember her embracing me when I came out of the anesthesia after my heart attack in 2008. Her words were that she didn't know what our future looked like, but whatever it was, it would be with us together. I repeat those words to her today that whatever our road may be, it will be us together.

She's told me recently that the thing that makes her the saddest is when she sees me sad for her. God has never put a more selfless person on this earth than my beautiful Sandy. My vow to her and to anyone who reads these words is that the vows we made to each other on that turnrow that December night so long ago are as true now as they were when we first made them. **We are forever!**

We've used the words of songwriters throughout the chapters of this book. I'm going to end my part of her memoir with the words of a song recorded by the group Alabama many years ago. It's one of Sandy's favorite songs. The words tell my love story and my passion for the girl with whom I've made my life's journey.

I'll admit I could feel it, the first time that we touched
And the look in your eyes, said you felt as much
But I'm not a man who falls too easily
It's best that you know just where you stand with me
'Cause I will give you my heart, faithful and true
And all the love it can hold, that's all I can do
And I've thought about, how long I'll love you
And it's only fair that you know, forever's as far as I'll go
When there's age around my eyes and gray in your hair
And it only takes a touch, to recall the love we shared

I won't take for granted you know my love is true
'Cause each night in your arms, I will whisper to you
'Cause I will give you my heart, faithful and true
And all the love it can hold, that's all I can do
And I've thought about, how long I'll love you
*And it's only fair that you know, **forever's as far as I'll go**

(Forever's as Far as I'll Go - Alabama)

I can't say it any better than that!

I'll love you forever, Sandy!

Lee J.

ABOUT THE AUTHORS

Sandy and Lee J. co-authored her memoir that chronicles her struggles to overcome her painful shyness and high-functioning anxiety as a child. Her suppression of many of her normal childhood emotions hid a persona deep within her psyche that only emerged after their marriage. Their time in the Air Force, as he became a fighter pilot and she served as an officer's wife, allowed her to discover her hidden side that she was completely unaware even existed.

www.ingramcontent.com/pod-product-compliance
Lightning Source LLC
Chambersburg PA
CBHW020438130626
46549CB00001B/196